Contents

- Thank & Special Mentions
- Introduction
- Time Differences Table
- Section 1 – Important Dates
  - The Turning of the Wheel (Sabbat Dates)
  - Lunar Eclipses
  - Solar Eclipses
  - Meteor Shower Dates
  - Retrograde Dates
- Section 2 – Month by Month Reference Calendar
- Section 3 -Zodiac Calendars
  - Traditional Astrology
  - Native American Zodiac
  - Celtic Animal Zodiac
  - Celtic Tree Zodiac
  - Chinese Astrology
  - Tibetan Zodiac
  - Aztec Zodiac
  - Egyptian Zodiac
- Section 4 – Days of the Week & Correspondences
- Section 5 – Birthstones
- Section 6 – Names of the Moon
- Section 7 – Appendix
  - Colour Magic
  - Metals Correspondences in Magic
- Section 8 – Resources & Recommended Books, Websites and Facebook Pages

Thanks & Special Mentions!

I have to start by thanking my awesome Fiancé, Russell. From helping me with what contents will go into the almanac to reminding me that I have a deadline when I have been procrastinating; he has been as important to the publishing process as I have. Thank you from the bottom of my heart Baba, without you this book would never have been born. My next thanks needs to go to Emily Kitazawa and Roger Quaintance. These are the people who have read the growing form of the Almanac; they have read each of the 43,000 plus words.

There is a large group of people who have supported me, through each and every page of this book. They are the ones who I am dedicating this book to. To every witch that has ever walked this path, or looked up to the moon and saw magic. I am sure I will forget someone, but I will do my best.

- Kelly Easton
- Danielle and Aaron Marshal;
- Karen Kasinskas
- Kerry Greenaway
- Cat West
- Cat Wilson
- Stephanie Butterworth
- Mary Breeden
- Derrie Carpenter
- Chuck and Laura Dunn
- Raphaela Awwad
- Emma Eastwood
- Rach Collins
- Eva Stocks
- Kiri Vengeance
- Nathan Smieja
- Shawn Robbins
- Joel Pusch

- Bella Leona
- Jen Austin
- Everyone at Magical Recipes Online
- Sunbow Pendragon
- Jess Howe
- Nicola Eaton

I also need to thank my mum for being just fantastic; supporting me through every phase of my life and spiritual development. Lastly; I want to thank my crazy familiar, Phoenix. She always has my back when she is whipping around like a bullet.

Introduction

Welcome to the Ramblings of a Rainbow Witch 2019 Almanac by Nixie Vale

What is an Almanac?

An almanac is an annual calendar or handbook containing information, important dates and general interest details on such topics as: astronomical data, year book, calendar, a compendium, planting and harvesting guide and astrological and lunar cycles.

What is the Purpose of the almanac?

My goal is to create a concise, down to earth book with information for witches, wiccans and pagans with as little bias as possible. I have been blessed with the gift of a wordsmith and a passion for my path and spiritual journey.

I began my path way back in the mast millennium (okay it was 1999, but hey...) and the love of learning and the knowledge I gained never left me. I began my writing journey on various online forums and in 2012 I created Ramblings of Rainbow Witch with the love and support of a close-knit group of friends. Over the last 6 years I have been blessed to meet many wonderful people, they have shared the same love for the craft as I, and allowed me to grow as a writer and a witch.

As I write this introduction Ramblings of a Rainbow Witch, has 60,740 fans and the group has 6,600 members; which still boggles my mind. It's because of the love and support of each and every soul that gave me the courage to write this book. It's YOUR love and support.

What's New?
This year the RoaRW almanac is bigger and better, and each page is jam packed with juicy information or all of your witchy needs. I have done more research, read more books and made more notes than ever before to bring you something wonderful for everyone. I wanted to create something that is both useful and beautiful, a book that a novice and a veteran will enjoy.

The Year of the Pig
2019 is the Year of the Pig/Boar according to Chinese Astrology. The Year of the Pig has fallen in the years 1935, 1947, 1959, 1971, 1983, 1995 and 2007; it will also fall in the following years 2019 (obviously), 2031 and 2043.

In Chinese Astrology the Pig/Boar is always
the last sign of the cycle begins again. The
year of the Pig/Boar always follows the year of
the Dog, and precedes the year of the Rat.
The Pig is the last sign of the Chinese Zodiac
because (s)he was the last to arrive at a great
meeting headed by the Jade Emperor or the
Buddha (depending on the source).

The Pig is a mild mannered, lucky animal that
represents a carefree and fun nature that is
blessed with good fortune. Those born in the
Year of the Pig are happy, easy going, honest,
trusting, sincere and brave. They are
considerate, responsible, independent and
optimistic. They are also stubborn, naive,
quick-tempered and materialistic but who
doesn't have a dark side.

Correspondences of the Pig
- Earthly Branch – Hai
- Energy – Yin
- Element – Water = Shui
- Lucky Flowers – Hydrangea, Pitcher
  Plant
- Lucky Crystal – Ruby
- Lucky Numbers – 2, 5 and 8
- Lucky Colours – Yellow, Grey, Brown
  and Gold
- Lucky Directions – Southeast and
  Northeast
- Unlucky Numbers – 1, 3 and 9
- Unlucky Colours – Red, Blue and
  Green
- Unlucky Directions – East and West.

⏲ Time Differences ⏲

All of the times in this book are GMT and this table will show how far behind or ahead countries are according to GMT.

United Kingdom – London – Greenwich Mean Time (GMT)

Country	Capital City	+ or – GMT
Afghanistan	Kabul	+4 hours ahead
Argentina	Buenos Aires	-3 hours behind
Algeria	Algiers	+1 hours ahead
Australia	Canberra	+ 8 to +10 hour ahead
Austria	Vienna	+1 hour ahead
Bangladesh	Dhaka	+7 hours ahead
Belize	Belmopan	-6 hours behind
Belgium	Brussels	+1 hour ahead
Bermuda	Hamilton	-3 hours behind
Botswana	Gaborone	+2 hours ahead
Brazil	Brasilia	-2 to -4 hours behind
Cambodia	Phnom Penh	+7 hours ahead
Canada	Ottawa	-3 to -9 hours behind
Chile	Santiago	-4 hours behind
China	Beijing	+8 hours ahead
Congo	Brazzaville	+1 hour ahead
Costa Rica	San Jose	-6 hours behind
Denmark	Copenhagen	+1 hour ahead
Dominican Republic	Santo Domingo	-4 hours behind
Egypt	Cairo	+3 hours ahead
Fiji	Suva	+ 12 hours ahead
Finland	Helsinki	+2 hours ahead

France	Paris	+1 hour ahead
Gambia	Banjul	0 hours - GMT
Germany	Berlin	+1 hour ahead
Greece	Athens	+2 hours ahead
Greenland	Nuuk	-2 hours behind
Guatemala	Guatemala City	-6 hours behind
Guernsey	Saint Peter Port	+1 hour ahead
Haiti	Port-au-Prince	-5 hours behind
Iceland	Reykjavik	0 Hours – GMT
India	New Delhi	+5 hours ahead
Ireland	Dublin	0 Hours – GMT
Israel	Jerusalem	+3 hours ahead
Italy	Rome	+1 hour ahead
Jamaica	Kingston	-5 hours behind
Japan	Tokyo	+9 hours ahead
Kenya	Nairobi	+3 hours ahead
Libya	Tripoli	+2 hours ahead
Luxembourg	Luxembourg	+1 hour ahead
Malawi	Blantyre	+2 hours ahead
Malta	Valetta	+1 hour ahead
Mexico	Mexico City	-6 to -8 hours behind
Mongolia	Ulaanbaatar	+7 to +8 hours behind
Mozambique	Maputo	+2 hours ahead
Netherlands	Amsterdam	
New Zealand	Auckland	+12 hours ahead
Norway	Oslo	+1 hours ahead
Oman	Muscat	+4 hours ahead
Pakistan	Islamabad	+5 hours ahead
Peru	Lima	-5 hours ahead
Poland	Warsaw	+2 hours ahead
Portugal	Lisbon	0 hours – GMT
Puerto Rico	San Juan	-4 hours behind
Romania	Bucharest	+3 hours ahead
Russia	Moscow	+3 to +12 hours ahead
Saint Lucia	Castries	-4 hours behind
Samoa	Apia	-11 hours behind

South Africa	Pretoria	+2 hours ahead
Spain	Madrid	+1 hour ahead
Sweden	Stockholm	+1 hour ahead
Switzerland	Berne	+1 hour ahead
Tanzania	Dodoma	+3 hours ahead
Thailand	Bangkok	+7 hours ahead
Uganda	Kampala	+3 hours ahead
USA	Washington DC	-5 to -11 hours behind
Uruguay	Montevideo	-3 hours behind
Virgin Islands	Charlotte Amalie	-4 hours behind
Zambia	Lusaka	+2 hours ahead
Zimbabwe	Harare	+2 hours ahead

You can find more information about your own time zone and how many hours ahead or behind you are using these websites:

- www.timeanddate.com
- www.countries-ofthe-world.com
- www.timezoneconverter.com
- www.geoips.com

Section 1
Important Dates

This section is dedicated to all of the important dates throughout the year; from the festivals of the Wheel of the Year to the dates of planetary Retrogrades and Meteor Showers. All of these dates will appear in the calendar section as well so you can easily keep track of the dates.

The Turning of the Wheel
Festivals; Celebrations and Feasts.

I have began with Imbolc as it is the first celebration in the year for the Northern Hemisphere, and for those in the Southern Hemisphere the year begins with Lughnasadh.

Imbolc

What is Imbolc?

When the Wheel of the Year turns to Imbolc and the return of the Sun. Imbolc is also known as Candlemas and the Feast of Bridget. Imbolc is one of the Celtic Fire Festivals and commemorates the changing of the Goddess from her Crone phase into her Maiden phase. Imbolc celebrates the coming of spring, when the first signs of new growth emerges from the long winter sleep.

Im-molc or Em-bowl'g – Major Sabbat, High Holiday, Fire Festival.
1st or 2nd of February or when the Sun reaches 15 degrees in Aquarius (Northern Hemisphere)
1st or 2nd August or when the Sun reaches 15 degrees in Libra (Southern Hemisphere)

AKA: Imbolg, Candlemas, Brigantia, Festival of Light, Brigid's Day, La Fheill, An Fheill Bride, Candelaria, Chinese New Year, Lupercalia (15th), Groundhog Day.

Correspondences for Imbolc

Essence & Meaning: Conception, Initiation, Insight, Mirth, Creativity, Inspiration, Renewal, Dedication, Breath of Life, Life's Path, Wise-Counsel, Plans, Preparation, Growth of the Sun God, First Stirring of Mother Earth, Mid-Winter, Lambing Season, Honouring the Virgin or Maiden Goddesses, Festival of Light. Purification, Renewal, Creative Expression & Inspiration, Feast of Milk and Bread, Re-lighting the Hearth, Seeking Omens of spring and Telling Stories.

Animals/Mythical Beings: Phoenix, Dragon, Firebird, Deer, Groundhog, Ewes, Robins, Sheep, Lambs and animals waking from hibernation.

Crystals: Amethyst, Garnet, Onyx, Turquoise, Selenite, Quartz.

Incense: Jasmine, Rosemary, Frankincense, Cinnamon, Neroli, Musk, Olive, Sweet Pea, Basil, Myrrh, Wisteria and Carnation

Colour: Brown, Pink, Red, Orange, White, Lavender, Pale Yellow and Silver

Symbols/Tools/Decorations: White Flowers, Marigolds, Plum Blossom, Snowdrops, Daffodils, Brigid's Wheel, Brigid's Cross, Candles – a red or white candle in a cauldron of earth, Earth Doll or Corn Dolly, Bride's Bed, Broom, Milk, Birchwood, Snowflakes, Evergreens, Homemade Besoms.

Goddesses: Virgin Goddesses, Diana, Venus, Aradia, Athena, Innanna, Vesta, Gaia, the "Maiden" of the Triple Goddess, Brigid, Selene and Branwen.

God: Young Sun God, Pan, Cernunnos, Herne, Cupid, Eros, Drumuzi.

Food: Dairy Products, Spicy Foods, Cake, Waffles, Pancakes, Herbal Tea, Poppy Seed Bread or Cakes.

Herbs: Angelica, Basil, Bay, Benzoin, Celandine, Clover, Heather, Myrrh and Willow.

Element: Earth

Gender: Female

Time of Day: Midnight

Ostara

What is Ostara?

The Spring Equinox is a time of celebration. Some people begin to enjoy the lengthening days and the warming of the air. Work begins in the garden with the planting of flower beds and vegetable gardens. At Ostara we begin to connect to nature as she begins to wake. Ostara is also known as the Vernal Equinox, a point when nature is in balance.

Oh-star-ah, Lesser Sabbat, Spring/Vernal Equinox
21st or 22nd March or when the Sun enters Aries (Northern Hemisphere)
21st to 23rd September or when the Sun enters Libra (Southern Hemisphere)

AKA: Ostre, Eostre, Rites of Spring, Eostre's Day, Lady Day, First Day of Spring, Easter, Alban Eiler, Bacchanalia.

Correspondences for Ostara

Essence/Meaning: Strength, Birthing, Completion, Power, Love, Sexuality, Embodiment of Spirit Fertility, Opening, Beginnings, the God Comes of Age, Balance of Light and Dark, Plant & Animal Fertility, Sowing Seeds, Invention, New Growth, New Projects, Seed & Planting Blessings and Planting.

Animals/Mythical Beings: Unicorn, Merfolk, Pegasus, Rabbits, Hares, Chicks, Swallows, Snakes and baby animals in general

Crystals: Rose Quartz, Moonstone, Amethyst, Aquamarine, Bloodstone, Red Jasper.

Incense: Violet, Lotus, Jasmine, Rose, Marigold, Sage, Lavender, Narcissus, Ginger, Broom.

Colours: Pastel Colours in general, Gold, Pale Green, Grass Green, Blue, Lemon Yellow, Pale Yellow and Pale Pink.

Tools/Symbols/Decorations: Coloured Eggs, Baskets, Nests, Equilateral Cross, Butterfly,

Cocoons, Sprouting Plants, Violets, Wildflowers, Lambs, Hares and Rabbits.
Goddesses: Eostre, Ostara, Kore, Isis, Astrate, Ishtar, Minerva, Maiden Goddesses, Lady of the Lake, Young Goddesses.
Gods: Hare, the Green Man, Taliesin, Dagda, Cernunnos, Pan, Adonis, Young & Warrior Gods.
Foods: Fish, Sweets, Hot Cross Buns, Sweet Breads, Cakes, Eggs, Honey or Maple Syrup Cakes, Seasonal Fruits, Milk and Punch.
Herbs: Celandine, Tansy, Cinquefoil, crocus, Dogwood, Daffodil, Honeysuckle, Iris, Jasmine, Rose, Hyssop, Liden, Violet.
Element: Air
Gender: Masculine
Time of Day: Dawn

Beltane

What is Beltane?

Beltane is the second of the four Celtic Fire Festivals and fire plays a pivotal role at Beltane. Beltane is sometimes known as May Day. May is the time when the Earth is at its most fertile and some traditions describe how the Great Mother (the goddess) and her Consort (the horned God) unite and from this union new life comes forth.

Beel-teen, Bell-Tayn – Major Sabbat, High Holiday, Fire Festival.
30th April to 1st May or when the Sun is 15 degrees in Taurus
31st October or when the Sun is 15 degrees in Libra

AKA: Bhealtainn, Bealtaine, Lady Day, Samhredh, La Baal Tinne, May Eve, May Day, Walspurgis Night, Rudemas, Shenn do Boaldyn.

Correspondences for Beltane
Essence/Meaning: Compassion, Youthful, Playfulness, Sensuality, Sexuality, Lust, Passion, the Arrival of the Tuatha de Dannan to Ireland,

the Union of the God and Goddess, Love,
Romance, Fertility Magic and Faery Magic.
Offerings to the Elements, Crop Blessings,
Relighting Sacred Fires, Divination, Building &
creating Sacred Spaces, Honouring House and
Home Spirits or Guardians, Dancing around a
Maypole, Jumping a Balefire, Frolicking in Fields,
The Great Rite – Literal or Symbolic Union
Animals/Mythical Beings: White Cow, Goat,
Giants, Honey Bees, Faeries, Satyrs, Fawns,
Pegasus and Rabbit.
Crystals: Emerald, Carnelian, Sapphire, Rose
Quartz, Lapis Lazuli, Yellow Agate, Bloodstone
Incense: Passion Flower, Frankincense, Tuberose,
Vanilla, Lilac, Rose.
Colours: Red, Orange, Yellow, Gold, Green, Blue,
White and Silver
Tools/Symbols/Decorations: Maypole, Ribbons,
Flowers, Flower Crowns, Bowers, White Flowers,
Daisy Chains, White Wine, Fire, Balefires, Chalice
& Athame, Seasonal Fruit and Vegetables.
Goddesses: May Queen, Flora, Maia, Floral
Goddesses, Aphrodite, Blodewedd, Erzulie, Baubo,
Rhea, Prithvi.
Gods: May King, the Horned God, Herne,
Cernunnos, the Green Man, Bel, Ba'al, Gods of the
Hunt.
*****Beltane is the Union of the God and the Goddess;
this can be represented literally, or symbolically.***
Foods: Dairy, Honey, Oats, Red Fruits, Salads,
Red or Rose Wine, Meat, Sweet Treats, Cakes,
Almonds.
Herbs: Angelica, Damina, Hawthorn, Hibiscus,
Saffron, Ash Tree, Bluebell, Cinquefoil, Daisy,
Frankincense, Ivy, Lilac, Marsh Marigold,
Meadowsweet, Primrose, Rose, Satyrion Root,
Woodriff, Cowslip, Yarrow.
Element: Air
Gender: Masculine
Time of Day: Dawn

Litha

What is Litha?

Litha is also known as the Summer Solstice, the point when the sun is at its strongest. It's also the point where the days are at their longest. We celebrate the strength of the Sun and the growth of the crops planted earlier in the year. In some traditions this is the time of year where the Oak and Holly Kings do battle. The Holly King is the Victor and with that comes the darkening of the days and the decline of the light.

Leet-th-a – Lesser Sabbat, Longest Day, Summer Solstice
21st June or when the Sun enters Cancer (Northern Hemisphere)
21st December or when the Sun enters Capricorn (Southern Hemisphere)

AKA: Midsummer, Letha, Feill Sheathain, Alban Hefin, Alban Heruin, Mid-Summer's Eve, St John's Eve, Feast of Epona.

Correspondences for Litha

Essence/Meaning: Fire, the Sun, Partnership, Nourishment, Fertilisation, Crowning of the Sun God, Death of the Sun God, End of the Ordeal of the Green Man, Honouring the Solar Deities, Honouring the Pregnant Goddess, Spirit & Fae Healing, Planetary Healing, Divination, Honouring the Battle between the Holly and Oak King, Early Harvest, the Start of the Harvest Season.

Animals/Mythical Beings: Wren, Robin, Horses, Cattle, Satyrs, Faeries, Firebirds, Phoenix, Dragons and Thunderbirds.

Crystals: Lapis Lazuli, Diamond, Carnelian, Tiger's Eye, Jade, Emerald, Aventurine, Yellow Topaz, Yellow Calcite, Citrine, Golden Calcite.

Incense: Heliotrope, Saffron, orange, Frankincense, Myrrh, Wisteria, Cinnamon, Mint, Rose, Lemon, Lavender, Pine and Sandalwood.

Colours: Blue, Green, Yellow, Orange, Red and Gold

Tools/Symbols/Decorations: the Sun, Oak, Birch & Fir Branches, Sunflowers, Lilies, Red, Yellow or

Golden Flowers, Love Amulets, Sea Shells,
Summer Fruits, Flower and Feather Wreaths, Sun
Wheel, Fire, Circle of Stones, Sun Dials, Feathers,
Blades and Swords.
Goddesses: Mother Earth, Mother Nature, Venus,
Aphrodite, Yemaya, Astrate, Freya, Hathor, Isthar,
and other Goddesses of Love, beauty, Passion and
the Sea.
Gods: Father Sky, the Oak King, the Holly King,
the Green Man, King Arthur and other Solar Gods.
Food: Fresh fruit and Vegetables, Lemons,
Oranges, Pumpernickel, Bread, Ale, Wine, Carrots
and Orange Juice.
Herbs: Anise, Mugwort, Chamomile, Rose, Wild
Roses, Oak Blossom, Lily, Cinquefoil, Lavender,
Fennel, Elder, Hemp, Thyme, Larkspur, Nettle,
Wisteria, Vervain, St John's Wart, Heartsease,
Rue, Fern, Wormwood, Pine, Heather, Yarrow, Oak
and Holly Trees.
Element: Fire
Gender: Masculine
Time of Day: Dusk or Dawn

Lughnasadh

What is Lughnasadh?

Lughnasadh is also known as Lammas which Loaf
Mass and is the first of the harvest festivals. It is
the harvest of the corn, wheat and grains. What
grew from the seeds you sown earlier in the year?
This is the time when we realise that summer will
soon be coming to an end. Lughnasadh is the
Festival for the Celtic God Lugh while for others it
is the first or earliest harvest.

Loo-nas-ah – Major Sabbat, High Holiday, Fire
Festival, First Harvest.
1st to 2nd August or when the Sun is 15 degrees in
Leo (Northern Hemisphere)
1st to 2nd February or when the Sun is 15 degrees
in Aquarius (Southern Hemisphere)

AKA: Lunasa, Lughnasaad, First Harvest, Feast of
Cardens, Feast of Bread, Tailltean Games, Teltain
Cornucopia, Ceresalia, Lammas, Elembious,
Festival of the Green Corn

Correspondences for Lughnasadh

Essence/Meaning: fruitfulness, Reaping what you
have Sown, Harvesting, Harvest Festival, Making
and Offering Loaves of Bread, Horn of Plenty,
Cauldron of Plenty, Astrology, Prosperity,
Generosity, Abundance, Baking Bread, Dancing
around the Corn Mother, Harvesting and Drying
Herbs and Feasting.

Animals/Mythical Beings: Griffon, Basilisk,
Rooster, Calves, Centaurs, Firebird and Phoenix.

Crystals: Aventurine, Citrine, Peridot, Sardonyx,
Yellow Diamonds.

Incense: Ale, Rose, Rose Hips, Rosemary,
Chamomile, Eucalyptus, Safflower, Corn,
Passionflower, Frankincense and Sandalwood.

Colour: Red, Orange, Golden Yellow, Green Light
Brown, Gold, Bronze and Grey.

Tools/Symbols/Decorations: Corn, Cornucopia,
Red or Yellow Flowers, Sheaves of Corn, Wheat,
Barley, Seasonal Fruits and Vegetables, Corn
Dollies, Bread, Cauldron, Sickle, Scythe, other
Threshing Tools, Seasonal Herbs and Phallic
Symbols.

Goddesses: Mother Nature, Dana, Tailltiu,
Demeter, Ceres, Seelu, Isis, the Corn Mother,
Luna and other Agricultural Goddesses.

Gods: Lugh, Lleu, Dagon, Tammuz, Dummuzi,
Dionysus, Tanus, Taranus.

Foods: Loaves of Homemade Bread – Wheat, Oats,
Corn, Barley, Cakes, Potatoes, Summer Squash,
Nuts, Acorns, Wild Berries, Apples, Rice, Pears,
Pies, Wine, Crab Apples, Tea, Grapes, Cider, Ale,
Beer and Mead.

Herbs: Grain, Acacia, Ginseng, Sloe, Cornstalks,
Cyclamen, Aloe, Sunflower, Hollyhock, Myrtle.

Element: Fire

Gender: Feminine

Time of Day: Noon

Mabon

What is Mabon?

Mabon is the time of year when night and day are once again equal; it's the mirror the Ostara. The scales of time begin to favour the darkness. Mabon is when we give thanks for the Sun and the abundance of crops. This is the time when then Goddess moves away from her Mother phase into her Crone phase while her consort prepares for his death. Mabon is the second and predominant harvest festival and one of the most common symbols for Mabon is the Apple. Mabon is also known as the Autumnal Equinox.

May-bon, May-bun, Ma-Bawn – Lesser Sabbat, Fall/Autumnal Equinox.
21st to 23rd September or when the Sun enters Libra (Northern Hemisphere)
21st to 23rd March or when the Sun enters Aries (Southern Hemisphere)

AKA: Michaelmas, the Second Harvest Festival, Witches' Thanksgiving, Harvest Home, Feast of Avalon, Festival of Dionysus.

Correspondences for Mabon

Essence/Meaning: Beauty, Joy, the Fullness of Life, Harvest of the Year's Desires, Strength, Laughter, Power, Prosperity, Equality, Balance, Appreciation, Harvest, Protection, Wealth, Security, Death of the God, Assumption of the Crone, Balance of Light and Dark, the Second Harvest Festival, Offerings to the Land, Offerings to the Fae (especially Gnomes), Honouring the Spirit World, Past Life Recall, Making Wine, Harvesting and Feasting on Seasonal Produce, Gathering Seed Pods and Drying them.
Animals/Mythical Beings: Dogs, Wolves, Stags, Blackbird, Owl, Salmon, Goat, Gnomes, Sphinx, Minotaur, Cyclops,

Crystals: Yellow Agate, Carnelian, Yellow Topaz, Citrine, Amber, Amethyst, Smoky Quartz.

Incense: Pine, Sweet-Grass, Apple, Apple Blossom, Benzoin, Myrrh, Frankincense, Jasmine, Sage, Aloe, Black Pepper, Patchouli, Cinnamon, Clove, Oak and Moss

Colours: Brown, green, Orange, Burgundy, Scarlet, Yellow, Copper, Bronze, Russet, Maroon, Indigo and Violet

Tools/Symbols/Decorations: Corn, Red Fruits, Autumnal Flowers, Poppies, Hazelnuts, Fallen Leaves, Acorns, Pinecones, Cypress Cones, Oak Sprigs, Pomegranates, Statues of the God and the Goddess, Mabon Wreaths, Vines, grapes, Gourd, Cornucopia, Horns and Cauldrons of Plenty, Marigolds, Sunflowers, Apples, Harvested Foods, Drums, Rattles, Sun Wheels, Sickle, Scythe, Baskets and Candles.

Goddesses: Modron, Bona Da, Mother Earth, the Mother phase of the Triple Goddess, Persephone, Demeter, Ceres, Morgana, Sake Woman, Epona, Pamona and the Muses.

Gods: Ap Modron, Father Sky, Dionysus, the Wicker Man, the Corn Man, Thoth, Hermes, Hotei, Thor, Bacchus and any other Aging Gods and Wine Gods.

Foods: Wheat products, Bread, Grains, Nuts, Berries, Grapes, Acorns, Seeds, Dried Fruits, Corn, Beans, Squash, Carrots, Onions, Figs, Apples, Potatoes, Hops, Sassafras, Pomegranates, Goose, Mutton, Wine, Ale, Cider and Mead.

Herbs: Myrrh, Thistle, Tobacco, Oak Leaves, Hazel, Hops, Acorns, Marigold, Rose, Sage, Milkweed, Solomon's Seal, Aster, Fern, Honeysuckle, Benzoin, Passionflower, Pine, Cedar, Ivy.

Element: Water

Gender: Feminine

Time of Day: Evening

Samhain

What is Samhain?

Samhain is actually pronounced Sow-In and is the last of the four Celtic Fire Festivals and the last of the Harvest festivals of the year, the time when preparations are being made for the winter months. Samhain is considered to be the most magical time of year as the veil between this world and the next thins, making communication with those who have passed easier. It is also the time when we honour all those have come before us and no longer with us.

Sow-en, Sow-in or Sow-een. Greater Sabbat, High Holiday, Fire Festival.

31st October to 1st November or when the Sun enters 15 degrees in Scorpio (Northern Hemisphere)

30th April to 1st May or when the Sun enters 15 degrees in Gemini (Southern Hemisphere)

AKA: Samhainn, Samonios, Hallow'een, Hallowmas, All Hallows Eve, All Saints Day, All Soul's Day, Dias de los Muertos, Day of the Dead, Celtic New Year, Witches' New Year, Trinoux Samonia, Shaowfest, Martinmas, Old Hallowmas, La Samha, Feile Moingfenne, Hallowtide, Oidhche na-h-aimileise, The Night of Mischief or Confusion, Oidhche Shamna.

Correspondences for Samhain

Essence/Meaning: Magic, Plenty, Knowledge, Wisdom, the Crone, the End of Summer, Honouring the Ancestors, Thinning and Lifting of the Veil, Change, Death, Transformation, Thinning between the Living and the Dead, Guidance, Divination, protection, Reincarnation, Honouring your Lost Loved Ones, Silent Suppers, Past Life Recall, Costumes, Final Harvest, Preparing for Winter, Feasting, Trick or Treat, Paying off the Debts of the Year.

Animals/Mythical Beings: Bats, Cats, Dogs, Pooka, Goblins, Gorgons (Medusa), Harpies. Spiders, Rats and Beansidhe.

Crystals: Jet, Obsidian, Onyx. Carnelian, Amethyst, Sodalite, Lapis Lazuli, Fire Agate, Amber, Red Jasper.

Incense: Frankincense. Basil, Yarrow, Camphor, Lilac, Clove, Rosewood, Wormwood, Dragon's Blood, Nag Champa, Patchouli, Heliotrope, Mint, Nutmeg, Sage, Ylang-ylang.

Colour: Black, Orange, Red, Purple, White, Gold, Silver Bronze.

Tools/Symbols/Decorations: Black Cloths, Oak Leaves, Acorns, Straw, Balefire, Besom, Black Cats, Bats, Spiders, Crescent Moons, Cauldrons, Pendulums, Crystal Balls, Scrying Mirrors, Tarot Cards, Oracle Cards, Candles, Jack 'o' Lanterns, Grains, Harvest Foods – Pumpkins, Squash, etc... Bare Branches, Skulls, Animal Bones, Antlers, Hazelwood, Pictures of Dead Loved Ones.

Goddesses: The Crone aspect of the Triple Goddess, Hecate, Cerridwen, Arianhod, Caillech, Baba Yaga, Al-Ilat, Bast(et), Hel, Kali, the Morrigan and other Goddesses of Death and the Underworld.

Gods: The Horned Hunter, Cernunnos, Pan, Osiris, Hades, Gwyn ap Nudd, Anubis, Coyote Brother, Loki, Dis, Arawn and other Gods of Death and the Underworld.

Foods: Apple, Pumpkin Pie, Pomegranate, Squash, Hazelnuts, Corn, Cranberry, Muffins, Bread, Ale, Cider, Herbal Tea.

Herbs: Allspice, Broom, Comfrey, Dandelion, Deadly Nightshade, Mugwort, Catnip, Dittany of Crete, Fern, Flax, Mandrake, Mullein, Dragons Blood, Sage, Straw, Thistles, Oak Leaf, Wormwood.

Element: Water

Gender: Masculine

Time of Day: Midnight.

Yule

What is Yule?

Yule is also known as the Winter Solstice and is the time when we celebrate the rebirth of the Sun. As with the Summer Solstice the Oak and Holly Kings once again do battle and this time the Oak King is the victor and this heralds the return of the Sun. For almost every religion, every tradition this is a time of year to gather with friends and family; celebrating good times, enjoying good food among good company

Ewe-el, Lesser Sabbat, Winter Solstice.

AKA: Jul, Saturnalia (17th to 15th), Yuletide, Midwinter, Fionn's Day, Alban Arthuan, Festival of Sol, Christmas (25th).

Correspondences for Yule

Essence/Meaning: Honour, Rebirth, Transformation, Light coming from Darkness, Creative Expression, the Mysteries, New Life, Regeneration, Reflection, Introspection, Death of the Holly King, Start of the Oak King's Reign, Start of the Trials of the Green Man, Death and Rebirth of the Sun God, the Shortest amount of Daylight of the Year, Honouring the triple Goddess, Birth of the Sun God and Jesus, Festival of Light, Personal Renewal, Honouring Friends and Family, Feasting, Singing, Dancing, Strengthening the Bonds of Friendship and Kinship, Generosity, Hanging Mistletoe, Apple Wassailing, Burning Candles, Bell Ringing, a Dawn Vigil.

Animals/Mythical Beings: Yule Goat (Nordic), Reindeer, Stag, Squirrel, Sacred White Buffalo, Chaos Monster, Kallikantzaroi-Ugly, Trolls, Phoenix, Elf, Gnome, Wren, Robin.

Crystals: Cat's Eye, Ruby, Garnet, Diamond, Bloodstone, Sapphire, Emerald.

Incense: Bayberry, Cedar, Cinnamon, Pine, Rosemary, Frankincense, Myrrh, Nutmeg, Ginger, Saffron, Wintergreen.

Tools/Symbols/Decorations: Bayberry, Candles, Evergreen Plants & Trees, Holly, Mistletoe, Poinsettia, Lights, Yule Log, Giving Gifts, Yule Tree, Spinning Wheel, Wreaths, Boughs, Snow,

Snowflakes, Bells, Berries, Mother & Child
Imagery.
Goddesses: Great Mother, Befana, Holda, Isis, the
Triple Goddess, the Virgin Mary, Tonazin, Lucina,
St Lucy, Bona Dea, Mother Earth, Eve, Opa, the
Snow Queen, Hertha, Frey, Frigga.
Gods: the Sun Child, Saturn, Cronos, Horus, Ra,
Jesus, Mithras, Balder, Odin (Santa Claus), the
Holly King, the Oak King, Sol, Invicta, Marduk,
Old Man Winter.
Foods: Various Nuts, Apples, Pears, Caraway
Cakes Soaked in Cider, Pork, Turkey, Stuffing,
Oranges, Cloves, Hibiscus or Ginger tea, Fruit
Cake, Dried Fruits, Cookies, Eggnog, Mulled Wine
Herbs: Blessed Thistle, Moss, Oak, Sage, Bay,
Bayberry, Cedar, Pine, Frankincense, Ginger,
Holly, Ivy, Juniper, Mistletoe, Myrrh, Rosemary,
Chamomile, Cinnamon, Valerian, Yarrow.
Element: Earth
Gender: Masculine
Time of Day: Dawn

Sabbat Dates and Times

The Sabbats are sacred feast days that many
Pagan, Spiritual and magical traditions celebrate
throughout the year. The Northern Hemisphere
has different dates to the Southern Hemisphere,
so I have included dates for both hemispheres in
the calendar section as well.
****Note** All times in this Almanac are UTC which is the
standard time that's commonly used across the world.
UTC stands for Coordinated Universal Time.**

Northern Hemisphere	Dates	Southern Hemisphere	Dates
Imbolc	1st February	**Imbolc**	1st August
Ostara	20th March at 21:58	**Ostara**	23rd September at 08:50
Beltane	1st May	**Beltane**	1st November

Litha	21st June at 16:54	Litha	21st December at 04:19
Lughnasadh	1st August	Lughnasadh	1st February
Mabon	23rd September at 08:50	Mabon	20th March at 21:58
Samhain	31st October	Samhain	31st April/1st May
Yule	21st December at 04:19	Yule	21st June at 16:54

Lunar and Solar Eclipses
Dates, Times and Where

2019 has five Eclipses; there will be three SOLAR eclipses and two LUNAR eclipses. Mercury will also pass in front of the Sun and this is called Mercury Transit.

Lunar Eclipses

From the Earth we experience three distinct kinds of Lunar eclipses; penumbral, partial and Total.

- **Penumbral Lunar Eclipse**

A Penumbral Lunar Eclipse happens when the moon passes through the faint outer part of the moon's shadow. As will all Lunar Eclipses, the Penumbral Lunar eclipses happen when the Earth moves between the Moon and the Sun, which means the Moon, cannot reflect the Sun's rays.

- **Partial Lunar Eclipse**

A Partial Lunar Eclipse occurs when part of the Moon passes through the darkest part of the

Earth's shadow, especially the cone-shaped region of full shadow cast by Earth, the Moon, or another body during an eclipse. Partial Lunar Eclipse is relatively easy to see even with the naked eye and the Moon may have a faint reddish colour.

- **Total Lunar Eclipse**

A Total Lunar Eclipse occurs when the whole moon passes through the darkest part of the Earth's shadow, especially the cone-shaped region of full shadow cast by Earth, the Moon, or another body during an eclipse. The Total Lunar Eclipse is the easiest Lunar Eclipse to see from Earth with the naked eye as the whole Moon's disk passes through and becomes a reddish-hue.

 # Lunar Eclipse Magic

For many Pagans all over the world the Moon is compelling and a vital part of their craft and this has been so for thousands of years. Over the centuries the Lunar Eclipse has become known as a harbinger of drastic changes or major events in a culture. Unlike the Solar Eclipse a Lunar Eclipse can be seen from most places in the world and can take on a reddish hue, which can appear to be a blood-like colour. Spells that are worked during a Lunar Eclipse have an amplified effect, and can end up having a whopping amount of power behind it. I have seen in groups and on pages that it is "dangerous" for a newbie to work spells during any kind of Eclipse, but I wouldn't say it's true, however if you feel you aren't ready or unsure about it, give it a miss. When you feel you're not ready, or unsure you will find your focus slipping and the spell can go awry.

- Spells for increasing psychic abilities, intuition and spiritual awareness are great for working during a Lunar Eclipse.

- The Lunar Eclipse spells and rituals for healing can be boosted by the energy of the Lunar Eclipse

- Rituals that connect you to the Lunar
  Deities such as Diana, Selene and Thoth

A Lunar Eclipse is a fantastic time to give offerings to the many Lunar Gods and Goddess, or to just a few.

Solar Eclipses

From the Earth we experience three distinct kinds of solar eclipses, total, partial and annular.

- **Total Eclipse**

A total eclipse occurs when the Moon completely covers the surface of the sun that is viewable from the Earth. A Total Eclipse can only be viewed from a limited area, and those outside of that area will probably only see a partial eclipse. The area that can see the Total Eclipse forms a belt which is usually around 100 miles wide by 10,000 miles long. The sky can darken during a total eclipse.

- **Partial Eclipse**

A partial eclipse is when only part of the moon obscures part of the sun disk. The sunlight isn't changed by the partial eclipse.

- **Annular Eclipse**

An annular eclipse occurs when the Moon passes in front of the Sun and visually appears smaller. When the moon passes across the sun disk, it passes across the centre which leaves a bright ring, which is known as an Annulus or a "ring of fire". The sky doesn't darken during an annular eclipse.

There is a rare kind of eclipse called a **Hybrid Eclipse** and this is when during the Moon's progress across the sun it changes from an annular eclipse to a total eclipse, or vice versa. I've not found too much information on the Hybrid Eclipse, or when the last one was.

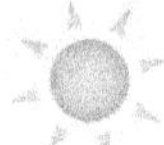 # Solar Eclipse Magic

The Solar Eclipse always happens at a New Moon, and this is often a time of rest and reflection, planning and looking inward. During a Solar Eclipse the Moon blocks out the light of the Sun, which is a powerful symbol of vitality and virility; a Solar Eclipse is a powerful and highly charged moment that can be felt radiating across the Earth, and this energy can bring big changes. These changes can be difficult, upsetting and very emotionally charges. They will start of slow and niggle at you before coming to a head at the Solar Eclipse; at this point you cannot ignore it these changes may be hard but at the core of your being it will make sense, even if it takes time.

During a Solar Eclipse we experience what is called a "micro-year" and this is when the Sun is whole, and is then partially or completely hidden and is once again visible once the eclipse is over. Within the short time it takes for the Moon to travel across the sun it we can experience a complete turn of the Wheel, passing through the Solstices and Equinoxes.

Eclipse	Date	Where can it be Seen?
Partial Solar Eclipse	Sunday 6th January	Eastern areas of Asia and the Pacific

Event	Date	Visible from
		Ocean
Total Lunar Eclipse	Monday 21st January	Europe, Asia, Africa, North America, South America, Pacific, Atlantic, the Indian Ocean and the Arctic
Total Solar Eclipse	Tuesday 2nd July	South and North America, Most areas of the southern tip of South America and the Pacific
Partial Lunar Eclipse	Tuesday 16th July	South and East Europe, Most of Asia, Australia, Africa, Southern and Eastern Areas of North America, South America, Pacific, Atlantic, Antarctica
Mercury Transit – Mercury passes in front of the Sun	Monday 11th November	South and West Europe, Most of Northern America, South America, Pacific, Atlantic, Great Britain, the Indian Ocean and Antarctica
Annular	Wednesday	East of

Solar Eclipse	26th December	Europe, Most of Asia, Northern and Western areas of Australia, Eastern areas of Africa, the Pacific and Indian Oceans

Meteor Shower Dates

A meteor shower is a fantastic celestial event where meteors shoot across the sky from any given point in the night skies. Meteor showers are caused when meteoroids enter the Earth's upper atmosphere and streak across the sky at extremely high speeds on varying but always parallel trajectories. Most of the meteors that appear in showers break up in the Earth's atmosphere and are harmless, never actually hitting the ground.

Quadrantis Meteor Shower	3rd and 4th January
Lyrids Meteor Shower	22nd and 23rd April
Eta Aquarids Meteor Shower	6th and 7th May
Delta Aquarids Meteor Shower	28th and 29th July
Perseid Meteor Shower	12th and 13th August
Draconids Meteor Shower	8th October
Orionids Meteor	21st and 22nd

Shower	October
Leonids Meteor Shower	17th and 18th November
Germids Meteor Shower	13th and 14th December
Ursids Meteor Shower	21st and 22nd December

Super Moon Dates

A Super Moon is a Full or New Moon that happens to coincide with the time when the Moon is closest to the Earth. The Moon's orbit around the Earth isn't perfectly round, it is actually elliptical, and the point where the Moon's orbit is closest to the Earth is called Perigee and the point where the Moon's Orbit is at its furthest is called Apogee.

Date	Moon Type	Time
Monday 21st January	Full Moon	05:16
Tuesday 19th February	Full Moon	15:53
Friday 16th October	New Moon	19:31

Retrograde Dates
Planetary and Celestial Retrograde Dates, Times and Signs

When a planet goes into retrograde there is an apparent change in its movement, they appear to move "backwards". Technically it's not moving backwards, it has just slowed down. It's our minds that make it appear to move backwards, like an optical illusion really, it's just hanging around the sun. We can't fully perceive these changes in the planet's movement so our eyes and brains do the best they can to make sense of it.

Jargon Buster of Retrograde

☐ *Enters Rx Zone – This is where the planet begins its path to retrograde*
☐ *Enters Retrograde – This is where the planet enters retrograde fully*
☐ *Goes Direct – This is where the planet returns to its normal movement*
☐ *Leaves Rx Zone - This is where the planet finishes its retrograde phase.*

Mercury

Mercury goes into retrograde three or four times a year, and each time is between nineteen and twenty-four days in length. In 2019 Mercury will go into retrograde three times.

Mercury governs communication; getting tongue-tied, being misunderstood and simply say the wrong things are all part of Mercury's Retrograde Phase. During this time it is prudent to check and double check all plans and arrangements because Mercury can, and will turn the best laid plans to dust; at times it just won't matter how organised you are, things can still go wrong. Mercury's retrograde phase has a reflective energy which can help you gain a new and different perspective; it can stop you mid-stride and make you think.

Mercury 1	Date	Time	Sign
Enters Rx Zone	19th February	08:19	Pisces
Enters Retrograde	5th March	12:15	Pisces
Goes Direct	28th March	08:53	Pisces
Leaves Rx Zone	16th April	18:04	Pisces

Mercury 2	Date	Time	Sign
Enters Rx Zone	20th June	12:11	Cancer
Enters Retrograde	7th July	18:10	Leo
Goes Direct	31st July	22:15	Cancer
Leaves Rx Zone	15th August	01:53	Leo

Mercury 3	Date	Time	Sign
Enters Rx Zone	11th October	17:51	Scorpio
Enters Retrograde	31st October	10:34	Scorpio
Goes Direct	20th November	13:09	Scorpio
Leaves Rx Zone	7th December	11:59	Scorpio

Venus

****No Retrograde Motion for Venus in 2019****

Venus goes into retrograde every eighteen months or so and lasts for about six weeks.

Venus is closely associated to matters of the heart, so it is the heart that can suffer the most during Venus' Retrograde phase. While Venus is in retrograde it is easy to get tempted by the dark side, and fall prey to the darker side of people or the darker side of their hearts. When Venus in Retrograde is a time you may try to cling to the relationships of your past whether they are healthy relationships or unhealthy. There is a vulnerable energy during this time and feel that you need a little more love, craving a little more attention. Sometimes people will feel shy about their feelings and feel uncomfortable about being open. Old flames can be re-lit but sometimes these old flames are in the past for a reason.

Mars

****No Retrograde Motion for Mars in 2019****

Mars goes into Retrograde about every twenty-six months and remains in Retrograde for fifty-five to eighty-eight days.

When Mars is in Retrograde the energy that has become characteristic with mars is being focused inwards rather than outwards. You may find that you are spending more time and energy looking back at different events from the past. Mars in Retrograde brings a strong pull to spiritual development at the price of other areas of your life being neglected. While Mars is in retrograde you may find that you are drawn to deep and thought provoking conversations can actually be bore stimulating and gratifying than sexual experiences – this is because the energy of Mars is being directed inwards.

Jupiter

Jupiter goes into Retrograde almost every year for around one hundred and twenty days.

Jupiter is the happy-go-lucky planet that encourages personal growth; however when

Jupiter enters Retrograde the energy becomes introspective turning this outward growth into inner discovery and spiritual development. While Jupiter is in its Retrograde phase is fantastic for spending time evaluating your personal integrity. During this time you may feel that your motivation disappears and your optimism for life drops away; this is because the "get-up-and-go" energy has stalled and won't have too much movement until Jupiter goes direct once again. The Jupiter Retrograde phase can help you become a better version of yourself.

Jupiter	Date	Time	Sign
Enters Rx Zone	14th January	03:29	Scorpio
Enters Retrograde	10th April	22:58	Scorpio
Goes Direct	11th August	11:59	Scorpio
Leaves Rx Zone	5th August	20:47	Scorpio

Saturn

Saturn goes into retrograde almost every year for around one hundred and forty days.

Saturn is the planet of self-discipline, and a powerful force driving us to reach for our goals; however when Saturn enters its retrograde phase you may feel that you are having to re-do everything that you have already done; feeling like you are actually doing twice the amount of work. You may experience feeling of doubt questioning your self-worth. When Saturn does go into Retrograde it can herald a time of spiritual development and spiritual maturity. Over your many lives you have had to learn and re-learn many things and this has brought you to a new and deeper spiritual strength. When Saturn goes into retrograde the discipline and rigidity breaks down; requiring you to "go with the flow".

Saturn	Date	Time	Sign
Enters Rx Zone	22nd January	09:04	Capricorn
Enters Retrograde	29th April	18:58	Capricorn
Goes Direct	18th September	02:13	Capricorn
Leaves Rx Zone	23rd January 2020	04:34	Capricorn

Uranus

Uranus goes into retrograde almost every for around one hundred and forty-eight days.

When Uranus is in Retrograde expect for there to be great awakenings. Some planets hold gentle energy while they are in Retrograde but you are out of luck when it comes to Uranus, it is a hard hitting energy that is very abrupt. Uranus won't capitulate until you face the changes that are facing you; there won't be any time outs either. This retrograde phase will show you what isn't working and what needs to change. Uranus will make you seek the answers to questions that you may not realise you wanted to ask. While Uranus is in Retrograde the energy will build and build until the only option is for it to explode it an eruption of energy. This intense energy can be difficult to navigate.

Uranus	Date	Time	Sign
Enters Rx Zone	24th April	20:56	Taurus
Enters Retrograde	11th August	18:10	Taurus
Goes Direct	10th	18:27	Taurus

	January 2020		
Leaves Rx Zone	26th April 2020	13:52	Taurus

Neptune

Neptune goes into Retrograde almost every year for around one hundred and fifty days.

When Neptune enters its Retrograde phase you can become more sensitive to all types of energy, making you receptive to both inward and outward stimuli. Neptune in its retrograde phase your perceptions become more acute and with this you may uncover problems and situations that you not have seen otherwise. When Neptune enters Retrograde it is essential that you pay attention to your inner voice and be aware of your sensitivity because you can become overloaded with the sensitivity of the energy. For Empaths it can be a very rough time, especially if they are surrounded by addictive personalities as you could become addicted to them. When Neptune is in Retrograde you could be influenced by paranoid making you question everything.

Neptune	Date	Time	Sign
Enters Rx Zone	28th February	13:55	Pisces
Enters Retrograde	21st June	04:56	Pisces
Goes Direct	27th November	03:48	Pisces
Leaves Rx Zone	16th March 2020	23:57	Pisces

Pluto

Pluto goes into retrograde almost every year, and remains in Retrograde for five to six months of the year

Pluto is the planetary force that can make you face the nastiest parts of yourself; it can be the greatest detective forging forward to find the answers you need. When Pluto is in Retrograde the energy is quite unpredictable which is an understatement. Unlike other planets when Pluto is in Retrograde Pluto's energy is clear and forward. It makes you look at situations and forces you to look inwards rather than looking to the outside. This is a time when you can sit and reflect on all areas of you life, even the parts of yourself that is kept hidden fro the world. Pluto in Retrograde will make you face your fears and conquer them.

Pluto	Date	Time	Sign
Enters Rx Zone	1st January	22:53	Capricorn
Enters Retrograde	24th April	08:05	Capricorn
Goes Direct	2nd October	21:42	Capricorn
Leaves Rx Zone	23rd January 2020	16:39	Capricorn

Celestial Bodies

Planets aren't the only celestial bodies that have a retrograde; other celestial bodies do too, such as Ceres, Chiron, Juno, Pallas and Vesta.

Juno – When Juno enters retrograde it is time to re-evaluate and take stock of your life and how you are communicating with others. Juno in Retrograde is a very detail orientated time and paying attention to the fine print and the exact details because they can easily be overlooked. While Juno is in retrograde you may find the courage to communicate with someone from your past. A time when you can set old wrongs right, apologising if it's necessary. Clear and honest communication is vital while Juno is in Retrograde.

Chiron – While Chiron is in Retrograde we can attract healing and guidance that we need most at this time. We are drawn to seek new ways of healing for the deepest part of our being. Chiron in Retrograde drives us to heal the places that we normally kept hidden, locked away from the light. This time helps to give us the courage and support to face this allowing the amazing transformational energy of Chiron in Retrograde.

Ceres – Ceres represents the nurturing abilities, family attachments and unconditional love. While Ceres is in Retrograde this nurturing energy will need to be focused outwards. It's time to let yourself feels what you so freely give to others. Ceres' retrograde phase teaches us to show yourselves unconditional love, fulfilling what you need, and this will inspire others to do the same.

Vesta When Vesta is in Retrograde it's time to bring yourself back the centre of your being, taking the time to focus your energy inwards. While Vesta is in retrograde it is a fantastic time to focus on your own sacred space – regardless of the form it takes. You will find new ways to amuse yourself while you are alone and you may even find your own creative muse.

Pallas Athene - When Pallas Athene is in retrograde it signals a time a time when we need to review our current social needs and even social reform. Pallas Athene in retrograde reminds you of what is necessary to incorporate feminine values into the existing social conventions and social systems.

Celestial Body	Retrograde Movement Begins	Retrograde Movement Ends
Ceres	18th April 2019	17th July 2019
Chiron	8th July 2019	12th December 2019
Juno	No Retrograde in 2019	No Retrograde in 2019
Pallas Athene	18th February 2019	30th May 2019
Vesta	23rd September 2019	29th December 2019

Section 2

The Month by Month Reference Calendar

In Section 3 you will find a Month by Month play of all the dates you will need for your own spiritual or pagan journey. This section will feature:

- The Moon's Journey Through the Zodiac Dates and Times
- Void of Course Dates and Times
- Full Moon Dates
- New Moon Dates
- Pagan Festival Dates
- Super Moon, and Black Moon Dates
- Retrograde Dates
- Zodiac Calendar Dates

- Eclipse Dates
- Harvesting/In Season Information
- Etc.......

The reason I am adding the dates in from the previous pages is so you can see how the energy is going to change and flow from month to month; which will help you prepare your magical workings.

Key for the Zodiac
NAZ = Native American Zodiac
TAZ = Traditional Astrological Zodiac
CAZ = Celtic Animal Zodiac
CTZ = Celtic Tree Zodiac
EZ = Egyptian Zodiac

January

What is in Season?

o Kale, Leeks, Cabbage, Cauliflower, Carrots and Swede are still staples from the garden. You may also notice some early signs of Purple Sprouting Broccoli.
o Well stored Apples, Pears, Beetroot, Onions, Garlic, Parsnips and Squash are going to be okay... but only if they are well stored.
o There is an abundance of imported food around too, so you can find foods such as Pineapple, Kiwi, Passion Fruit, and Bananas are available; even though they aren't "in season".
o You will still be able to find Black Truffles that have been imported too.
o Hare, Woodcock, Pheasant, and Venison are all in season and can be found in specialist butchers. Goose is another meat that is in season right now.

Birthstones for January

The classical Birthstone for January is **GARNET.**

The Birthstones for Capricorn are: ***RUBY, AGATE, GARNET, BLACK ONYX.***
The Birthstones for Aquarius are: ***GARNET, AMETHYST, OPAL, MOSS AGATE, and SUGILITE.***

Names of the Moon in January

- Colonial American- The Winter Moon
- Cherokee Native American – The Cold Moon
- Choctaw Native American – The Cooking Moon
- Sioux Native American – The Moon of the Terrible
- Celtic – The Quiet Moon
- English – The Wolf Moon
- Neo-Pagan – The Ice Moon

January 2019	
1st January TUESDAY	• New Years Day • Time of the Nile Begins • Pluto enters Rx Zone at 22:53 in Pisces • VOC starts at 22:36
2nd January WEDNESDAY	• The Moon enters Sagittarius at 08:58 • VOC ends at 08:58
3rd January THURSDAY	
4th January FRIDAY	• VOC starts at 17:41 • The Moon enters Capricorn at 18:54 • VOC ends at 18:54
5th January SATURDAY	

6th January SUNDAY	• The **New Moon** in Capricorn at 01:28 • Partial Solar Eclipse at 01:41

January 2019	
7th January MONDAY	• VOC Starts at 06:20 • The Moon enters Aquarius at 06:45 • VOC Ends at 06:45 • The Time of the Nile Ends
8th January TUESDAY	• The Time of Amon Ra Begins
9th January WEDNESDAY	• VOC Starts at 16:42 • The Moon enters Pisces at 19:43 • VOC Ends at 19:43
10th January THURSDAY	
11th January FRIDAY	• VOC Starts at 14:42
12th January SATURDAY	• The Moon enters Aries at 08:17 • VOC Ends at 08:17
13th January SUNDAY	

January 2019	
14th January MONDAY	• The Moon enters its First Quarter at 06:45 in Aries • VOC Starts at 15:55 • The Moon enters Taurus at 18:31 • VOC Ends at 18:31 • Pluto enters Rx Zone at 04:00 in Sagittarius
15th January TUESDAY	
16th January WEDNESDAY	• VOC Starts at 18:33
17th January THURSDAY	• The Moon enters Gemini at 01:00 • VOC Ends at 01:00
18th January FRIDAY	
19th January SATURDAY	• VOC Starts at 01:32 • The Moon enters Cancer at 03:43 • VOC ends at 03:43 • The Time of Capricorn Ends • The Time of the Goose Ends
20th January SUNDAY	• The Time of Aquarius Begins • The Time of the Otter Begins • The Time of the Stag Ends • The Time of Birch Ends

January 2019	
21st January MONDAY	• VOC Starts at 01:49 • The Moon enters Leo at 03:54 • VOC Ends at 03:54 • Total Lunar Eclipse at 05:12 • The **Full Moon** in Leo at 05:12

	• The Time of the Cat Begins • The Time of Rowan Begins • The Time of Amon Ra Ends
22nd January TUESDAY	• Saturn enters Rx Zone at 09:04 in Capricorn • The Time of Mout Begins
23rd January WEDNESDAY	• VOC Starts at 01:19 • The Moon enters Virgo at 03:21 • VOC Ends at 03:21
24th January THURSDAY	• VOC Starts at 13:50
25th January FRIDAY	• The Moon enters Libra at 04:02 • VOC Ends at 04:02
26th January SATURDAY	
27th January SUNDAY	• VOC Starts at 05:20 • The Moon enters Scorpio at 07:30 • VOC Ends at 07:30 • The Moon enters its Last Quarter at 21:10 in Scorpio

January 2019	
28th January MONDAY	• VOC Starts at 22:38
29th January TUESDAY	• The Moon enters Sagittarius at 14:32 • VOC Ends at 14:32
30th January WEDNESDAY	

31st January THURSDAY	<ul><li>VOC Starts at 22:32</li><li>The Time of Mout Ends</li></ul>

February

What is in Season?

o Seafood such as Shellfish, Clams, Cockles, and Muscles are in season this month.

o The Blood Orange has a very short seasonal period and February is when they are at their best and in season.

o Once again you will be able to find a plethora of imported foods such as Pineapple, Kiwi, and Pomegranates; but February is when are at their absolute best and of course they are plentiful to boot

o Leeks, Cabbages and Kale are still going strong; but they may look at little battered. They are still good though.

o Purple Sprouting Broccoli is growing spectacularly.

o The imported Black Truffles are still coming in from Italy.

o This is the last month Venison will be available at butchers

o If you still have well stored fruits and vegetables, they will still be good.

Birthstones for February

The Traditional Birthstone for February is
AMETHYST
The Birthstone for Aquarius include **GARNET, AMETHYST, OPAL, MOSS AGATE, SUGILITE**
The Birthstones for Pisces include
AMETHYST, AQUAMARINE, MOONSTONE,

BLOODSTONE, JADE, ROCK CRYSTAL, and
SAPPHIRE.

Names for the Moon in February
- Colonial American – The Trappers Moon
- Cherokee Native American – The Bony Moon
- Choctaw Native American – The Little Famine Moon
- Sioux Native American – The Moon of the Racoon
- Celtic – The Moon of Ice
- English – The Storm Moon
- Neo-Pagan – The Snow Moon

February 2019	
1st February FRIDAY	- **Imbolc** (Northern Hemisphere) - **Lughnasadh** (Southern Hemisphere) - The Moon enters Capricorn at 00:46 - VOC Ends at 00:46 - The Time of Amon Ra Begins
2nd February SATURDAY	
3rd February SUNDAY	- VOC Starts at 10:52 - The Moon enters Aquarius at 13:02 - VOC Ends at 13:02 -

February 2019	
4th February MONDAY	- The **New Moon** in Aquarius at 21:03

5th February	• VOC Starts at 23:58
TUESDAY	
6th February	• The Moon enters Pisces at 02:01 • VOC Ends at 02:01
WEDNESDAY	
7th February	• VOC Starts at 22:13
THURSDAY	
8th February	• The Moon enters Aries at 14:33 • VOC Ends at 14:33
FRIDAY	
9th February	
SATURDAY	
10th February	• VOC Starts at 23:47
SUNDAY	

February 2019	
11th February MONDAY	• The Moon enters Taurus at 01:28 • VOC Ends at 01:28 • The Time on Amon Ra Ends
12th February TUESDAY	• The Moon enters its First Quarter at 22:26 in Taurus • VOC Starts at 22:26 • The Time of Geb Begins
13th February WEDNESDAY	• The Moon enters Gemini at 09:31 • VOC Ends at 09:31
14th February	

THURSDAY	
15th February FRIDAY	• VOC Starts at 12:48 • The Moon enters Cancer at 14:02 • VOC Ends at 14:02
16th February SATURDAY	
17th February SUNDAY	• VOC Starts at 14:17 • The Moon enters Leo at 15:20 • VOC Ends at 15:20 • The Month of the Cat Ends • The Month of Rowan Ends

February 2019	
18th February MONDAY	• Pallas Athene Enters Retrograde • The Month of the Snake Begins • The Month of Ash Begins • The Month od Aquarius Ends • The Month of the Otter Ends
19th February TUESDAY	• VOC Starts at 13:50 • The Moon enters Virgo at 14:46 • VOC Starts at 14:46 • The **Full Moon** in Virgo at 15:53 • Mercury enters Rx Zone at 08:19 in Pisces • The Month of Pisces Begins • The Month of the Wolf Begins
20th February WEDNESDAY	Hehehe Today is my Birthday lol
21st February THURSDAY	• VOC Starts at 01:51 • The Moon enters Libra at 14:17 • VOC Ends at 14:17
22nd February	

FRIDAY	
23rd February SATURDAY	• VOC Starts at 15:10 • The Moon enters Scorpio at 15:55 • VOC Ends at 15:55
24th February SUNDAY	

February 2019	
25th February MONDAY	• VOC Starts at 12:13 • The Moon enters Sagittarius at 21:19 • VOC Ends at 21:19
26th February TUESDAY	• The Moon enters its Last Quarter at 11:27 in Sagittarius
27th February WEDNESDAY	
28th February THURSDAY	• VOC Starts at 06:17 • The Moon enters Capricorn at 06:47 • VOC Ends ay 06:47 • Neptune enters Rx Zone at 13:55 in Pisces • The Time of Geb Ends

<u>March</u>

What is in Season?

- ○ March sees the end of season for Brussels, so harvest them while you can.

- o Purple Sprouting Broccoli and Rhubarb are in abundance right now, and all harvests will be plentiful.
- o Storing Onions and Winter Lettuce are all showing new shoots and new growth which means they are ready for harvesting.
- o Shellfish like Muscles and Oysters are still in season, but they will soon be coming to their end.
- o Halibut, Cod, Coley and Sole are coming into season right now.
- o Sheep's and Goat's cheese is fantastic right now, and I dare say, maybe at its best.

Birthstones for March

The Birthstone for March is **AQUAMARINE**
The Birthstones for Pisces include **AMETHYST, AQUAMARINE, MOONSTONE, BLOODSTONE, ROCK CRYSTAL, and SAPPHIRE, JADE.**
The Birthstones for Aries include **DIAMOND, AQUAMARINE, BLOODSTONE,** and **JASPERS.**

Names of the Moon in March

- Colonial American – The Fish Moon
- Cherokee Native American – The Windy Moon
- Choctaw Native American – The Big Famine Moon
- Sioux Native American – The Moon when eyes are sore from Bright Snow
- Celtic – The Moon of Winds
- English – The Chaste Moon
- Neo-Pagan – The Death Moon

March 2019	
1st March FRIDAY	• The Time of Osiris Ends
2nd March	• VOC Starts at 18:47 • The Moon enters Aquarius at 19:06

SATURDAY	• VOC Ends at 19:06
3rd March SUNDAY	

March 2019

4th March MONDAY	
5th March TUESDAY	• VOC Starts at 08:05 • The Moon enters Pisces at 08:15 • VOC Ends at 08:15 • Mercury enters Retrograde at 12:15 in Pisces
6th March WEDNESDAY	• The **New Moon** in Pisces at 16:03
7th March THURSDAY	• VOC Starts at 19:08 • The Moon enters Aries at 20:27 • VOC Ends at 20:27
8th March FRIDAY	
9th March SATURDAY	• VOC Starts at 17:13
10th March SUNDAY	• The Moon enters Taurus at 07:09 • VOC Ends at 07:09 • The Time of Osiris Ends

March 2019	
11th March MONDAY	• The Time of Isis Begins
12th March TUESDAY	• VOC Starts at 09:30 • The Moon enters Gemini at 15:47 • VOC Ends at 15:47
13th March WEDNESDAY	
14th March THURSDAY	• The Moon enters its First Quarter at 10:26 in Gemini • VOC Starts at 12:30 • The Moon enters Cancer at 21:49 • VOC Ends at 21:49
15th March FRIDAY	
16th March SATURDAY	• VOC Starts at 18:02
17th March SUNDAY	• The Moon enters Leo at 00:56 • VOC Ends at 00:56 • The Month of the Snake End • The Month of Ash Ends

March 2019	
18th March MONDAY	• VOC Starts at 15:18 • The Month of the Fox Begins • The Month of Alder Begins
19th March TUESDAY	• The Moon enters Virgo at 01:41 • VOC Ends at 01:41

20th March WEDNESDAY	• VOC Starts 15:21 • **Ostara at 21:58** (Northern Hemisphere) • **Mabon at 21:58** (Southern Hemisphere) • The Month of the Wolf Ends
21st March THURSDAY	• The Moon enters Libra at 01:27 • VOC Ends at 01:27 • The **Full Moon** in Libra at 01:47 • The Month of the Falcon Begins • The Month of Pisces Ends
22nd March FRIDAY	• VOC Starts at 18:10 • The Month of Aries Begins
23rd March SATURDAY	• The Moon enters Scorpio at 02:16 • VOC Ends at 02:16
24th March SUNDAY	

March 2019	
25th March MONDAY	• VOC Starts at 02:23 • The Moon enters Sagittarius at 06:05 • VOC Ends at 06:05
26th March TUESDAY	
27th March WEDNESDAY	• VOC Starts at 02:36 • The Moon enters Capricorn at 14:07 • VOC Ends at 14:07
28th March THURSDAY	• The Moon enters its Last Quarter at 04:49 in Capricorn • Mercury Goes Direct at 08:53 in Pisces

29th March FRIDAY	
30th March SATURDAY	- VOC Starts at 00:04 - The Moon enters Aquarius at 01:45 - VOC Ends at 01:45
31st March SUNDAY	- The Time of Isis Ends

<u>April</u>

What is in Season?

- Seafood like Halibut, Crab and Salmon are now coming into season, and they will join the Shrimp and Lobster in their bounty.
- The last of the Purple Sprouting Broccoli is now ready to harvest and soon its season will pass.
- Peas and early Radishes are starting to come through.
- The first harvests of Asparagus, Rocket and Spring Onions, Watercress and Wild Nettles can be found if you are lucky.
- Rhubarb is plentiful, and you can pull in quite the bounty.
- Spring Lamb is now coming into season, and it will be the south west (of England) that will lead the trend.

Birthstones for April

The Birthstone for April is **DIAMOND**
The Birthstones for Aries include **DIAMOND, BLOODSTONE, JASPERS,** and **TOPAZ**.

The Birthstones for Taurus include ***AMBER, SAPPHIRE, CORAL, EMERALD***, and ***ROSE QUARTZ***

Names of the Moon in April

- Colonial America – The Trappers Moon
- Cherokee Native American – The Flower Moon
- Choctaw Native American – The Wildcat Moon
- Sioux Native American – The Moon when Geese Return in Scattered Formation
- Celtic – The Growing Moon
- English – The Seed Moon
- Neo-Pagan – The Awakening Moon

April 2019	
1st April MONDAY	• VOC Starts at 04:01 • The Moon enters Pisces at 15:47 • VOC Ends at 15:47 • The Time of Thoth Begins
2nd April TUESDAY	
3rd April WEDNESDAY	• VOC Starts at 16:35
4th April THURSDAY	• The Moon enters Aries at 03:56 • VOC Ends at 03:56
5th April FRIDAY	• The **New Moon** in Aries at 09:50
6th April SATURDAY	• VOC Starts at 03:14 • The Moon enters Taurus at 14:06 • VOC Ends at 14:06

7th April SUNDAY	

April 2019	
8th April MONDAY	• VOC Starts at 09:28 • The Moon enters Gemini at 22:14 • VOC Ends at 22:14 • Ceres Enters Retrograde
9th April TUESDAY	
10th April WEDNESDAY	• VOC Starts at 18:26 • Jupiter enters Retrograde at 11:17 in Sagittarius
11th April THURSDAY	• The Moon enters Cancer at 04:31 • VOC Ends at 04:31
12th April FRIDAY	• The Moon enters its First Quarter at 20:05 in Cancer
13th April SATURDAY	• VOC Starts at 00:32 • The Moon enters Leo at 08:50 • VOC Ends at 08:50
14th April SUNDAY	• The Month of the Fox Ends • The Month of Alder Ends

April 2019	
15th April	• VOC Starts at 21:38

MONDAY	<ul><li>The Moon enters Virgo at 11:13</li><li>VOC Ends at 11:13</li><li>The Month of the Cow Begins</li><li>The Month of Willow Begins</li></ul>
16th April TUESDAY	<ul><li>Mercury Leaves Rx Zone at 18:04 in Pisces</li></ul>
17th April WEDNESDAY	<ul><li>VOC Starts at 05:29</li><li>The Moon enters Libra at 12:21</li><li>VOC Ends at 12:21</li></ul>
18th April THURSDAY	
19th April FRIDAY	<ul><li>The **Full Moon** in Libra at 12:12</li><li>VOC Starts at 12:12</li><li>The Moon enters Scorpio at 13:40</li><li>VOC Ends at 13:40</li><li>The Time of Thoth Ends</li><li>The Month of Aries Ends</li><li>The Month of the Falcon Ends</li></ul>
20th April SATURDAY	<ul><li>The Time of Horus Begins</li><li>The Month of Taurus Begins</li><li>The Month of Beaver Begins</li><li></li></ul>
21st April SUNDAY	<ul><li>VOC Starts at 12:43</li><li>The Moon enters Sagittarius at 16:59</li><li>VOC Ends at 16:59</li></ul>

April 2019	
22nd April MONDAY	
23rd April	<ul><li>VOC Starts at 12:43</li><li>The Moon enters Capricorn at 23:49</li></ul>

TUESDAY	• VOC Ends at 23:49
24th April WEDNESDAY	• Pluto enters Retrograde at 08:05 in Capricorn • Uranus enters Rx Zone at 20:56 in Taurus • VOC Starts at 20:47
25th April THURSDAY	• The Moon enter Aquarius at 10:27 • VOC Ends at 10:27
26th April FRIDAY	
27th April SATURDAY	
28th April SUNDAY	• VOC Starts at 10:43 • The Moon enters Pisces at 23:11 • VOC End at 23:11

April 2019	
29th April MONDAY	• Saturn enters Retrograde at 18:58 in Capricorn
30th April TUESDAY	• VOC Starts at 22:57 • **Beltane Begins** (Northern Hemisphere) • **Samhain Begins** (Southern Hemisphere)

<u>May</u>

What is in Season?

- o Asparagus, Sorrel, Peas, Broad Beans, Radishes, Chives (and their flowers) and Young Spinach are just some of the treats to be had in May.
- o Globe Artichokes are at their best when they are small; they are quick to grow more, so there is no harm in harvesting them small.
- o New Potatoes are at the height of their season right now and can be sound in green grocers, markets and supermarkets.
- o Rhubarb is still alive and kicking well, bountiful and plentiful.
- o Strawberries can be seen this month as they begin to come into season.
- o Crabs, Sardines, Plaice and Mackerel are all bountiful this month.

Birthstones

The Birthstone for April is **DIAMOND.**
The Birthstones for Taurus include; **SAPPHIRE, AMBER, CORAL, EMERALD & ROSE QUARTZ.**
The Birthstones for Gemini include; **AGATE, CHRYSOPRASE, CITRINE, MOONSTONE, PEARL, & WHITE SAPPHIRE.**

Names for the Moon in May

- Colonial American – The Milk Moon
- Cherokee Native American – The Planting Moon
- Choctaw Native American – The Panther Moon
- Sioux Native American – The Moon when leaves are Green
- Celtic – The Bright Moon
- English – The Hare Moon
- Neo-Pagan – The Grass Moon

May 2019	
1st May WEDNESDAY	• The Moon enters Aries at 11:23 • VOC Ends at 11:23 • **Beltane** (Northern Hemisphere) • **Samhain** (Southern Hemisphere)
2nd May THURSDAY	
3rd May FRIDAY	• VOC Starts at 09:47 • The Moon enter Taurus at 21:17 • VOC Ends at 21:17
4th May SATURDAY	• The **New Moon** in Taurus at 23:45
5th May SUNDAY	• VOC Starts at 16:10

May 2019	
6th May MONDAY	• The Moon enters Gemini at 04:39 • VOC Ends at 04:39
7th May TUESDAY	
8th May WEDNESDAY	• VOC Starts at 00:49 • The Moon enters Cancer at 10:06 • VOC Ends at 10:06 • The Time of Horus Ends
9th May THURSDAY	• The Time of Anubis Begins

10th May FRIDAY	<ul><li>VOC Starts at 03:05</li><li>The Moon enters Leo at 14:13</li><li>VOC Ends at 14:13</li></ul>
11th May SATURDAY	
12th May SUNDAY	<ul><li>The Moon enters its First Quarter at 02:12 in Leo</li><li>VOC Starts at 13:24</li><li>The Moon enters Virgo at 17:21</li><li>VOC Ends at 17:21</li><li>The Month of the Cow Ends</li><li>The Month of Willow Ends</li></ul>

May 2019	
13th May MONDAY	<ul><li>The Month of the Seahorse Begins</li><li>The Month of Hawthorn Begins</li></ul>
14th May TUESDAY	<ul><li>VOC Starts at 18:18</li><li>The Moon enters Libra at 19:50</li><li>VOC Ends at 19:50</li></ul>
15th May WEDNESDAY	
16th May THURSDAY	<ul><li>VOC Starts at 10:37</li><li>The Moon enters Scorpio at 22:25</li><li>VOC Ends at 22:25</li></ul>
17th May FRIDAY	
18th May SATURDAY	<ul><li>The **Full Moon** in Scorpio at 22:11</li><li>VOC Starts at 22:11</li></ul>

19th May	• The Moon enters Sagittarius at 02:20
	• VOC Ends at 02;20
SUNDAY	

May 2019	
20th May	• VOC Starts at 18:04
	• The Month of Taurus Ends
MONDAY	• The Month of the Beaver Ends
21st May	• The Moon enters Capricorn at 08:56
	• VOC Ends at 08:56
TUESDAY	• The Month of Gemini Begins
	• The Month of the Deer Starts
22nd May	
WEDNESDAY	
23rd May	• VOC Starts at 04:57
	• The Moon enters Aquarius at 18:49
THURSDAY	• VOC Ends at 18:49
24th May	
FRIDAY	
25th May	• VOC Starts at 13:50
SATURDAY	
26th May	• The Moon enters Pisces at 07:07
	• VOC Ends at 07:07
SUNDAY	• The Moon enters its Last Quarter at 17:33 in Pisces

May 2019	
27th May MONDAY	• The Time of Anubis Ends
28th May TUESDAY	• VOC Starts at 05:20 • The Moon enters Aries at 19:31 • VOC Ends at 19:31 • The Time of Seth Begins
29th May WEDNESDAY	
30th May THURSDAY	• VOC Starts at 16:07 • Pallas Athene Leaves Retrograde
31st May FRIDAY	• The Moon enters Taurus at 05:42 • VOC Ends at 05:42

June

What is in Season?

o   Herbs such as Basil, Mint, and Dill are bountiful right now and ready for harvesting.

o   Fruits like Strawberries, Cherries, Raspberries and Apricots are at their best right now, so dig in and harvest some luscious fruit.

o   We are starting to see the first signs of the currents right now (Black, White and Red).

o   June is the time for Broad Beans, French Beans, Peas, Lettuce, Fennel and Carrots to come into season and they are all delicious.

o New Potatoes, Watercress, Spring Onions, and Radishes are all ready for a nice plentiful harvest.
o Crab, Sardines and Mackerel are in abundance right now, some say at their best, and they can be found at most fishmongers.
o Fresh and un-matured cheeses such as Feta and Ricotta are at their finest.

Birthstones

The Birthstone for June is **PEARL**
The Birthstones for Gemini include; ***AGATE, CHRYSOPRASE, CITRINE, MOONSTONE, PEARL & WHITE SAPPHIRE***
The Birthstones for Cancer include; ***EMERALD, MOONSTONE, PEARL & RUBY***

Names for the Moon in June

- Colonial American – The Rose Moon
- Cherokee Native American – The Green Corn Moon
- Choctaw Native American – The Windy Moon
- Sioux Native American – The Moon when the Berries are Ripe
- Celtic – The Moon of Horses
- English – The Dyan Moon
- Neo-Pagan – The Planting Moon

June 2019	
1st June SATURDAY	• VOC Starts at 23:52
2nd June SUNDAY	• The Moon enters Gemini at 12:47 • VOC Ends at 12:47

June 2019	
3rd June MONDAY	• The **New Moon** in Gemini at 11:01
4th June TUESDAY	• VOC Starts at 16:41 • The Moon enters Cancer at 17:16 • VOC Ends at 17:16
5th June WEDNESDAY	
6th June THURSDAY	• VOC Starts at 15:10 • The Moon enters Leo at 20:15 • VOC Ends at 20:15
7th June FRIDAY	
8th June SATURDAY	• VOC Starts at 22:23 • The Moon enters Virgo at 22:44 • VOC Ends at 22:44
9th June SUNDAY	• The Time of the Seahorse Ends • The Time of Hawthorn Ends

June 2019	
10th June MONDAY	• The Moon enters its First Quarter at 06:59 in Virgo • VOC Starts at 13:01 • The Time of the Wren Begins • The Time of Oak Begins
11th June TUESDAY	• The Moon enters Libra at 01:28 • VOC Ends at 01:28

12th June WEDNESDAY	• VOC Starts at 16:15
13th June THURSDAY	• The Moon enters Scorpio at 05:02 • VOC Ends 05:02
14th June FRIDAY	• VOC Starts at 20:45
15th June SATURDAY	• The Moon enters Sagittarius at 10:02 • VOC Ends at 10:02
16th June SUNDAY	

June 2019	
17th June MONDAY	• The **Full Moon** in Sagittarius at 09:30 • VOC Starts at 09:30 • The Moon enters Capricorn at 17:13 • VOC Ends at 17:13
18th June TUESDAY	• The Time of Seth Ends
19th June WEDNESDAY	• VOC Starts at 12:18 • The Time of the Nile Begins
20th June THURSDAY	• The Moon enters Aquarius at 03:00 • VOC Ends at 03:00 • Mercury enters Rx Zone at 12:11 in Cancer • The Month of Gemini Ends

	• The Month of the Deer Ends
21st June FRIDAY	• VOC Starts at 15:01 • Neptune Enters Retrograde at 04:56 in Pisces • The Month of Cancer Begins • The Month of the Woodpecker Begins • **Litha – Summer Solstice at 16:54** (Northern Hemisphere) • **Yule – Winter Solstice at 16:54** (Southern Hemisphere)
22nd June SATURDAY	• The Moon enters Pisces at 15:01 • VOC Ends at 15:01
23rd June SUNDAY	

June 2019	
24th June MONDAY	
25th June TUESDAY	• VOC Starts at 15:01 • The Moon enters Aries at 03:37 • VOC Ends at 03:37
26th June WEDNESDAY	
27th June THURSDAY	• VOC Starts at 08:51 • The Moon enters Taurus at 14:31 • VOC Ends at 14:31
28th June FRIDAY	• The Time of the Nile Ends

| 29th June

SATURDAY	• VOC Starts at 19:38 • The Moon enters Gemini at 22:08 • VOC Ends at 22:08
30th June

SUNDAY | |

<u>July</u>

What is in Season?

- o July is when the fruit season really kicks into full swing, and it is a bountiful bonanza. Apricots, Peaches, Nectarines, Cherries, Raspberries, various Currents, Gooseberries, Blueberries, Strawberries.... and the list goes on.
- o If you are lucky you may find Blackberries, Plums, Loganberries, and Tayberries out and about because they are starting to ripen and some are ready to pick.
- o Much like the fruit, vegetables are in full swing and are ready to bust at the seams. New Potatoes, Carrots, Salad Leaves, Runner Beans, Peas, Asparagus, Artichokes, Mongetout, Spring Onions, French beans, Celery, Lettuce and Rocket are all ready for harvest. July really is an excellent month.
- o July sees the end of the Broad Beans, but if you are very lucky you may find what is left for this season.
- o The Summer Herbs are at their best; Mint, Dill and Basil are among them.
- o Courgette (Zucchini) Flowers and Nasturtium are types of edible flowers that are available right now, making your plate all the more colourful.

- Sea Bass, Crab, Mackerel, and Sardines are plentiful during July.
- Young Cheeses are at their best because the milk is produced from animals that are eating fresh grass filled with nutrients.

Birthstones

The Birthstone for July is Ruby.

The Birthstones for Cancer include; ***EMERALD, MOOSTONE, PEARL, & RUBY.***

The Birthstones for Leo include; ***ONYX, CARNELIAN, SARDONYX, GOLDEN TOPAZ, TOURMALINE.***

Names for the Moon in July

- Colonial American – The Summer Moon
- Cherokee Native American – The Ripe Corn Moon
- Choctaw Native American – The Crane Moon
- Sioux Native American – The Moon of the Middle Summer
- Celtic – The Moon of Claiming
- English – The Rose Moon
- Neo-Pagan – The Rose Moon

July 2019	
1st July MONDAY	• VOC Starts at 22:47
2nd July TUESDAY	• The Moon enters Cancer at 02:23 • VOC Ends at 02:23 • The **New Moon** in Cancer at 20:16 •
3rd July WEDNESDAY	• VOC Starts at 15:24
4th July	• The Moon enters Leo at 04:19 • VOC Ends at 04:19

THURSDAY	
5th July **FRIDAY**	• VOC Starts at 07:42
6th July **SATURDAY**	• The Moon enters Virgo at 05:25 • VOC Ends at 05:25
7th July **SUNDAY**	• VOC Starts at 17:50 • Mercury enters Retrograde at 18:10 in Leo • The Month of the Wren Ends • The Month of Oak Ends

July 2019	
8th July MONDAY	• The Moon enters Libra at 07:06 • VOC Ends at 07:06 • Chiron enters Retrograde • The Month of the Horse Begins • The Month of Holly Begins
9th July TUESDAY	• The Moon enters its First Quarter at 11:54 in Libra • VOC Starts at 20:35
10th July WEDNESDAY	• The Moon enters Scorpio at 10:28 • VOC Ends at 10:28
11th July THURSDAY	
12th July FRIDAY	• VOC Starts at 01:28 • The Moon enters Sagittarius at 16:04 • VOC Ends at 16:04
13th July SATURDAY	• The Time of Anubis Ends

14th July	• VOC Start at 02:30
SUNDAY	• The Time of Bastet Begins

July 2019	
15th July MONDAY	• The Moon enters Capricorn at 00:04 • VOC Ends at 00:04
16th July TUESDAY	• There will be a PARTIAL Solar Eclipse at 22:30 • The **Full Moon** in Capricorn at 22:38 • VOC Starts at 22:38
17th July WEDNESDAY	• The Moon enters Aquarius at 10:18 • VOC Ends at 10:18 • Ceres Leaves Retrograde
18th July THURSDAY	• VOC Starts at 16:53
19th July FRIDAY	• The Moon enters Pisces at 22:18 • VOC Ends at 22:18
20th July SATURDAY	
21st July SUNDAY	• The Month of the Woodpecker Ends

July 2019

22nd July MONDAY	• VOC Starts at 09:34 • The Moon enters Aries at 11:02 • VOC Ends at 11:02 • The Month of the Salmon Begins • The Month of Cancer Ends
23rd July TUESDAY	• The Month of Leo Begins
24th July WEDNESDAY	• VOC Starts at 15:47 • The Moon enters Taurus at 22:42 • VOC Ends at 22:42
25th July THURSDAY	• The Moon enters its Last Quarter at 02:17 in Taurus
26th July FRIDAY	
27th July SATURDAY	• VOC Starts at 05:27 • The Moon enters Gemini at 07:28 • VOC Ends at 07:28
28th July SUNDAY	• VOC Starts at 16:23 • The Time of Bastet Ends

July 2019	
29th July MONDAY	• The Moon enters Cancer at 12:30 • VOC Ends at 12:30 • The Time of Sekhmet Begins
30th July TUESDAY	
31st July	• VOC Starts at 04:32

WEDNESDAY	<ul><li>The Moon enters Leo at 14:18</li><li>VOC Ends at 14:18</li><li>Mercury Goes Direct at 22:5? In Cancer</li></ul>

August

What is in Season?

- During August Plums are at the very best, so get them while you can.
- The summer fruits have begun to wane, and the autumn fruits are starting to come into their own. Figs and Melons are starting to ripen.
- Blackcurrants, Redcurrants, Tayberries, Apricots, Peaches and Blueberries are bountiful.
- Early-ripening Apples and Pears can be picked and enjoyed; but they may need to be sweetened.
- There is still an abundance of treats to be had in the late summer; Sweetcorn, Tomatoes, Sweet Peppers, Chilli Peppers, Aubergines (Eggplant) will be joining the likes of Courgettes (Zucchini) Beetroot, Lettuce, Sorrel and Cucumbers.
- Elderberries and Crab Apples are starting to ripen in the hedgerows.
- Seafood that's in season this month includes Plaice, Mackerel, Sardines, Sole, Squid, Crab and Lobsters.
- Goat Meat is particularly good this month and coincides with festivals and Eid.

Birthstones

The Birthstone for August is Peridot.
The Birthstones for Leo include; ***ONYX, CARNELIAN, SARDONYX, GOLDEN TOPAZ, TOURMALINE.***
The Birthstones for Virgo include; ***CARNELIAN, JADE, JASPER, MOSS AGATE, SAPPHIRE.***

Names for the Moon in August

- Colonial American – The Dog Days Moon
- Cherokee Native American – The Fruit Moon
- Choctaw Native American – The Women's Moon
- Sioux Native American – The Moon when all Things Ripen
- Celtic – The Dispute Moon
- English – The Lightning Moon
- Neo-Pagan – The Lightning Moon

August 2019	
1st August THURSDAY	• The **New Moon** in Leo at 04:11 • VOC Starts at 21:47 • **Lughnasadh** (Northern Hemisphere) • **Imbolc** (Southern Hemisphere)
2nd August FRIDAY	• The Moon enters Virgo at 14:20 • VOC Ends at 14:20
3rd August SATURDAY	
4th August SUNDAY	• VOC Starts at 05:27 • The Moon enters Libra at 14:29 • VOC Ends at 14:29 • The Month of the Horse Ends • The Month of Holly Ends

August 2019	
5th August MONDAY	• The Month of the Fish Begins • The Month of Hazel Begins

6th August TUESDAY	• VOC Starts at 08:35 • The Moon enters Scorpio at 16:31 • VOC Ends at 16:31
7th August WEDNESDAY	• The Moon enters its First Quarter at 18:20 in Scorpio
8th August THURSDAY	• VOC Starts at 15:57 • The Moon enters Sagittarius at 21:34 • VOC Ends at 21:34
9th August FRIDAY	
10th August SATURDAY	• VOC Starts at 20:50
11th August SUNDAY	• The Moon enters Capricorn at 05:49 • VOC Ends at 05:49 • The Time of Sekhmet Ends • Uranus enters Retrograde at 18:10 in Taurus

August 2019	
12th August MONDAY	• VOC Starts at 23:11 • The Time of Horus Begins
13th August TUESDAY	• The Moon enters Aquarius at 16:35 • VOC Ends at 16:35
14th August WEDNESDAY	

15th August THURSDAY	• The **Full Moon** in Aquarius at 13:29 • Mercury Leaves Rx Zone at 01:53 in Cancer
16th August FRIDAY	• VOC Starts at 02:01 • The Moon enters Pisces at 04:49 • VOC Ends at 04:49
17th August SATURDAY	• VOC Starts at 23:34
18th August SUNDAY	The Moon enters Aries 17:32 • VOC Ends at 17:32

August 2019	
19th August MONDAY	• The Time of Horus Ends
20th August TUESDAY	• The Time of the Geb Begins
21st August WEDNESDAY	• VOC Starts at 05:06 • The Moon enters Taurus 05:36 • VOC Ends at 05:36 • The Month of the Salmon Ends
22nd August THURSDAY	• VOC Start at 22:32 • The Month of the Bear Begins • The Month of Leo Ends
23rd August FRIDAY	• The Moon enters Gemini at 15:33 • VOC Ends at 15:33 • The Moon enters its Last Quarter at 15:55 in Gemini • The Month of Virgo Begins
24th August	

SATURDAY	
25th August SUNDAY	• VOC Starts at 07:58 • The Moon enters Cancer at 22:05 • VOC Ends at 22:05

August 2019	
26th August MONDAY	
27th August TUESDAY	• VOC Stats at 09:55
28th August WEDNESDAY	• The Moon enters Leo at 00:53 • VOC Ends at 00:53
29th August THURSDAY	• VOC Starts at 01:06
30th August FRIDAY	• The Moon enters Virgo at 00:57 • VOC Ends at 00:57 • The New Moon in Virgo at 11:37 • The Black Moon in Virgo at 11:37 (Second New Moon in August)
31st August SATURDAY	• VOC Starts at 09:46 • The Time of Geb Ends

September

What is in Season?

o There is a wealth of fruits, vegetables and herbs in season right now, so much so that you are literally spoilt for choice. Let's break it down a little. 1) **Tomatoes** and **Aubergines** are at their best in September. The height of their season is very brief but it is outstanding. 2) All the Mediterranean vegetables are at their utmost best. 3) **Turnips, Leeks, Kale** and other Autumn and Winter vegetables are starting to come into season.

o Fruit that is at their best include **Plums, Blackberries, Apples, Pears** and **Raspberries;** all ready for those pies and crumbles.

o **Figs, Melons, Nectarines** and **Peaches** are plentiful at the moment, so make the most of their bounty.

o If you are someone that likes to forage then **Damsons, Elderberries** and **Blackberries** are abundant along and in hedgerows.

o **Parsley, Thyme, Basil, Coriander**, and **Oregano** are still to be had.

o **Grouse, Partridge, Duck, Goose** and **Guinea Fowl** are starting to come into season in September so keep your eyes open at butchers.

o **Crab, Scallops, Lobster, Hake, Megrim Sole, Sardines, Mackerel** and **Plaice** are ample under the waves at the moment.

Birthstones

The Birthstone for September is *SAPPHIRE.*
The Birthstones for Virgo include; *CARNELIAN, JADE, JASPER, MOSS AGATE, SAPPHIRE.*
The Birthstones for Libra include; *PERIDOT, LAPIS LAZULI, OPAL, CHRYSOLITE.*

Names of the Moon in September

- Colonial American - The Harvest Moon
- Cherokee Native American – The Nut Moon

- Choctaw Native American – The Mulberry Moon
- Sioux Native American – The Moon when the Calves Grow Hair
- Celtic – The Singing Moon
- English – The Barley Moon
- Neo-Pagan – The Harvest Moon

September 2019	
1st September SUNDAY	• The Moon enters Libra at 00:07 • VOC Ends at 00:07 • The Time of the Nile Begins • The Month of the Fish Ends • The Month of Hazel Ends

September 2019	
2nd September MONDAY	• VOC Starts at 09:33 • The Month of the Swan Begins • The Month of Vine Begins
3rd September TUESDAY	• The Moon enters Scorpio at 00:34 • VOC Ends at 00:34
4th September WEDNESDAY	• VOC Starts at 11:58
5th September THURSDAY	• The Moon enters Sagittarius at 04:10 • VOC Ends at 04:10
6th September FRIDAY	• The Moon enters its First Quarter at 04:10 in Sagittarius • VOC Starts at 17:03
7th September	• The Moon enters Capricorn at 11:37

SATURDAY	• VOC Ends at 11:37 • The Time of the Nile Ends
8th September SUNDAY	• The Time of Mout Begins

September 2019	
9th September MONDAY	• VOC Starts at 09:30 • The Moon enters Aquarius at 22:23 • VOC Ends at 22:23
10th September TUESDAY	
11th September WEDNESDAY	• VOC Starts at 06:22
12th September THURSDAY	• The Moon enters Pisces at 10:51 • VOC Ends at 10:51
13th September FRIDAY	
14th September SATURDAY	• The **Full Moon** in Pisces at 05:32 • VOC Starts at 05:32 • The Moon enters Aries at 23:32 • VOC Ends at 23:32
15th September SUNDAY	

<table>
<tr><td colspan="2" align="center">September 2019</td></tr>
<tr><td>16th September

MONDAY</td><td>•   VOC Starts at 17:02</td></tr>
<tr><td>17th September

TUESDAY</td><td>•   The Moon enters Taurus at 11:30
•   VOC Ends at 11:30</td></tr>
<tr><td>18th September

WEDNESDAY</td><td>•   Saturn Goes Direct at 02:13 in Capricorn</td></tr>
<tr><td>19th September

THURSDAY</td><td>•   VOC Starts at 14:56
•   The Moon enters Gemini at 21:57
•   VOC Ends at 21:57</td></tr>
<tr><td>20th September

FRIDAY</td><td></td></tr>
<tr><td>21st September

SATURDAY</td><td>•   The Month of the Bear Ends</td></tr>
<tr><td>22nd September

SUNDAY</td><td>•   The Moon enters its Last Quarter at 03:30
•   VOC Starts at 03:40
•   The Moon enters Cancer at 05:49
•   VOC Ends at 05:49
•   The Month of the Raven Begins
•   The Month of Virgo Ends
•   The Time of Mout Ends</td></tr>
</table>

<table>
<tr><td colspan="2" align="center">September 2019</td></tr>
<tr><td>23rd September

MONDAY</td><td>•   VOC Starts at 23:05
•   **Mabon** at 08:50 (Northern Hemisphere)
•   **Ostara** at 08:50 (Southern Hemisphere)
•   The Month of Libra Begins
•   Vesta enters Retrograde</td></tr>
</table>

	• The Time of Bastet Begins
24th September TUESDAY	• The Moon enters Leo at 10:19 • VOC Ends at 10:19
25th September WEDNESDAY	• VOC Starts at 17:13
26th September THURSDAY	• The Moon enters Virgo at 11:36 • VOC Ends at 11:36
27th September FRIDAY	• The Time of Bastet Ends
28th September SATURDAY	• VOC Starts at 04:57 • The Moon enters Libra at 11:02 • VOC Ends at 11:02 • The **New Moon** in Libra at 19:26 • The Time of Seth Begins
29th September SUNDAY	• The Month of the Swan Ends • The Month of Vine Ends

September 2019	
30th September MONDAY	• VOC Starts at 03:05 • The Moon enters Scorpio 10:41 • VOC Ends at 10:41 • The Month of the Butterfly Begins • The Month of Ivy Begins

<u>October</u>

What is in Season?

- Aubergines (Eggplant), Tomatoes and
  Chillies are coming to the end of their
  season, so if you want to harvest them, be
  quick before it is too late.
- There is plenty of **Beetroot, Carrots,
  Parsnips, Kale** and **Cabbage** around; the
  latter will grow no matter what the weather
  does.
- October is **Wild Mushroom** season and
  specialist shops and delis will have **Ceps**,
  and **Puffballs**, for example.
- **White Truffles** are coming into season this
  month
- This month is all about the tree fruits like
  Apples, Pears, Quinces and **Medlars.**
- **Grapes** are maintaining nicely and if you
  are lucky you may be able to find some
  Blackberries
- October is the start of the Hunting season;
  so this means you'll start to find **Duck,
  Goose, Grouse, Hare, Pheasant, Rabbit**
  and **Venison** in butchers and
  supermarkets.
- **Mackerel** is coming to the end of its
  season, so you will be lucky to find them in
  fishmongers. **Oysters** are quickly following
  suit so be quick.
- **Hake, Lemon Sole,** and **Sardines** are still
  in season and readily available.

Birthstones

The Birthstone for October is ***OPAL***.
The Birthstones for Libra include; ***PERIDOT,
LAPIS LAZULI, OPAL, CHRYSOLITE***
The Birthstones for Scorpio include; ***BERYL,
APACHE TEAR, AQUAMARINE, CORAL,
OBSIDIAN.***

Names of the Moon in October

- Colonial American - The Hunter's Moon

- Cherokee Native American – The Harvest Moon
- Choctaw Native American – The Blackberry Moon
- Sioux Native American – The moon when the Quilting and Beading is Done
- Celtic – The Harvest Moon
- English – The Blood Moon
- Neo-Pagan – The Blood Moon

October 2019	
1st October TUESDAY	
2nd October WEDNESDAY	<ul><li>VOC Starts at 10:45</li><li>The Moon enters Sagittarius 12:44</li><li>VOC Ends at 12:44</li><li>Pluto Goes Direct at 21:24 in Capricorn</li><li>The Time of Seth Ends</li></ul>
3rd October THURSDAY	<ul><li>The Time of Bastet Begins</li></ul>
4th October FRIDAY	<ul><li>VOC Starts at 08:33</li><li>The Moon enters Capricorn at 18:43</li><li>VOC Ends at 18:43</li></ul>
5th October SATURDAY	<ul><li>The Moon enters its First Quarter at 17:46 in Capricorn</li></ul>
6th October SUNDAY	

October 2019	
7th October MONDAY	• VOC Starts at 00:25 • The Moon enters Aquarius at 04:41 • VOC Ends at 04:41
8th October TUESDAY	• VOC Starts at 19:26
9th October WEDNESDAY	• The Moon enters Pisces at 17:05 • VOC Ends at 17:05
10th October THURSDAY	
11th October FRIDAY	• VOC Starts at 10:55
12th October SATURDAY	• The Moon enters Aries at 05:45 • VOC Ends at 05:45
13th October SUNDAY	• The **Full Moon** in Aries at 22:07 • VOC Starts at 22:58

October 2019	
14th October MONDAY	• The Moon enters Taurus at 17:23 • VOC Ends at 17:23
15th October TUESDAY	

16th October	• VOC Starts at 09:37
WEDNESDAY	
17th October	• The Moon enters Gemini at 03:29 • VOC Ends at 03:29 • The Time of Bastet Ends
THURSDAY	
18th October	• The Time of Isis Begins
FRIDAY	
19th October	• VOC Starts at 03:13 • The Moon enters Cancer at 11:42 • VOC Ends at 11:42
SATURDAY	
20th October	
SUNDAY	

October 2019	
21st October	• The Moon enters its Last Quarter at 13:39 in Cancer • VOC Starts at 13:39 • The Moon enters Leo at 17:28 • VOC Ends at 17:28
MONDAY	
22nd October	• The Month of Libra Ends • The Month of the Raven Ends
TUESDAY	
23rd October	• VOC Starts at 19:14 • The Moon enters Virgo at 20:29 • VOC Ends at 20:29 • The Month of Scorpio Begins • The Month of the Snake Begins
WEDNESDAY	
24th October	
THURSDAY	

25th October FRIDAY	• VOC Starts at 13:59 • The Moon enters Libra at 21:19 • VOC Ends at 21:19
26th October SATURDAY	
27th October SUNDAY	• VOC Starts at 08:21 • The Moon enters Scorpio 20:29 • VOC Ends at 20:29 • The Month of the Butterfly Ends • The Month of Ivy Ends

October 2019	
28th October MONDAY	• The **New Moon** in Scorpio at 03:38 • The Month of the Wolf Begins • The Time of Reed Begins •
29th October TUESDAY	• VOC Starts at 17:34 • The Moon enters Sagittarius at 21:58 • VOC Ends at 21:58 • The Time of Isis Begins
30th October WEDNESDAY	• The Time of Sekhmet Begins
31st October THURSDAY	• VOC Starts at 14:29 • Mercury enters Retrograde at 10:34 in Scorpio • **Samhain** (Northern Hemisphere) • **Beltane** (Southern Hemisphere)

November

What is in Season?

- o November is the time for the hardiest of vegetables, **Artichokes, Carrots, Beetroot, Cauliflower, Brussels, Kale, Winter Cabbage**, and **Borloth Beans** are among the seasonal favourites.
- o **Cranberries, Satsuma, Clementine** and **Pomegranates** are all coming into season this month; not to mention **Apples** and **Pears** can still be found.
- o **Nuts** are bountiful; **Hazelnuts, Chestnuts**, and **Walnuts** are ripe and ready.
- o **Wild Mushrooms** and **White Truffles** are still plentiful.
- o **Duck, Goose, Partridge, Pheasant** and **Venison** are well into their season and will be joined by **Pigeon**.
- o **Stilton Cheese** it at it's very best right now
- o **Sardines, Skate, Clams** and **Mussels** are all on the menu in November.

Birthstones

The Birthstone for November is ***TOPAZ***.
The Birthstones for Scorpio include; ***BERYL, APACHE TEAR, AQUAMARINE, CORAL, OBSIDIAN***.
The Birthstones for Sagittarius include; ***TOPAZ, AMETHYST, RUBY, SAPPHIRE, TURQUOISE***.

Names of the Moon for November

- Colonial American – The Beaver Moon
- Cherokee Native American – The Trading Moon
- Choctaw Native American – The Sassafras Moon
- Sioux Native American – The Moon when Horns are Broken
- Celtic – The Dark Moon
- English – The Snow Moon

- Neo-Pagan – The Tree Moon.

November 2019	
1st November FRIDAY	• The Moon enters Capricorn at 02:38 • VOC Ends at 02:38
2nd November SATURDAY	
3rd November SUNDAY	• VOC Starts at 05:46 • The Moon enters Aquarius at 11:19 • VOC Ends at 11:19

November 2019	
4th November MONDAY	• The Moon enter its First Quarter at 10:22
5th November TUESDAY	• VOC Starts at 14:36 • The Moon enters Pisces at 23:07 • VOC Ends at 23:07 • Jupiter leaves Rx Zone at 20:41 in Sagittarius
6th November WEDNESDAY	
7th November THURSDAY	• The Time of Sekhmet Ends
8th November FRIDAY	• VOC Starts at 01:12 • The Moon enters Aries at 11:48 • VOC Ends at 11:48 • The Time of Thoth Begins
9th November	

SATURDAY	
10th November SUNDAY	• VOC Starts at 14:00 • The Moon enters Taurus at 23:17 • VOC Ends at 23:17

November 2019	
11th November MONDAY	
12th November TUESDAY	• The **Full Moon** in Taurus at 13:34 • VOC Starts at 15:47
13th November WEDNESDAY	• The Moon enters Gemini at 08:45 • VOC Ends at 08:45
14th November THURSDAY	
15th November FRIDAY	• VOC Starts at 11:39 • The Moon enters Cancer at 16:14 • VOC Ends at 16:14
16th November SATURDAY	
17th November SUNDAY	• VOC Starts at 20:14 • The Moon enters Leo at 21:56 • VOC Ends at 21:56 • The Time of Thoth Ends

November 2019	
18th November MONDAY	• The Time of the Nile Begins
19th November TUESDAY	• The Moon enters its Last Quarter at 21:10 in Leo • VOC Starts at 21:10
20th November WEDNESDAY	• The Moon enters Virgo at 01:54 • VOC Ends at 01:54 • Mercury goes Direct at 13:09 in Scorpio
21st November THURSDAY	• The Month of Scorpio Ends
22nd November FRIDAY	• VOC Starts at 03:31 • The Moon enters Libra at 04:19 • VOC Ends at 04:19 • The Month Sagittarius Begins • The Month of the Snake Begins
23rd November SATURDAY	• The Month of the Owl Begins
24th November SUNDAY	• VOC Starts at 02:49 • The Moon enters Scorpio at 05:58 • VOC Ends at 05:58 • The Month of the Wolf Ends • The Month of Reed Begins

November 2019	
25th November MONDAY	• VOC Starts at 17:29 • The Month of the Falcon Begins • The Month of Elder Begins
26th November	• The Moon enters Sagittarius at 08:10 • VOC Ends at 08:10

UESDAY	• The New Moon in Sagittarius at 15:05 • The Time of the Nile Ends
7th November VEDNESDAY	• The Time of Osiris Begins • Neptune goes Direct at 03:48 in Pisces
8th November HURSDAY	• VOC Starts at 10:49 • The Moon enters Capricorn at 12:32 • VOC Ends at 12:32
9th November RIDAY	
0th November ATURDAY	• VOC Starts at 03:56 • The Moon enters Aquarius at 20:13 • VOC Ends at 20:13

December

What is in Season?

- **Artichokes, Carrots, Beetroot, Parsnips, Cauliflower, Brussels Sprouts, Kale** and **Winter Cabbage** are all going strong despite the cold.
- **Satsuma, Clementine,** and **Cranberries,** are now readily available in markets and shops.
- **Hazelnuts** and **Chestnuts** are bountiful this month.
- **Turkey** has come to the height of its season now, but you can also find **Duck, Goose, Grouse, Partridge, Pigeon** and **Venison**; which means you are spoilt for choice.
- **Stilton Cheese** is extra mature in December and has a delightful taste

- o **Sardines, Skate**, **Clams** and **Mussels** are still going strong, giving you plenty of choice.

Birthstones

The Birthstone for December is Turquoise
The Birthstones for Sagittarius include; ***TOPAZ, AMETHYST, RUBY SAPPHIRE, TURQUOISE.***
The Birthstones for Capricorn include; ***RUBY, AGATE, GARNET, ONYX.***

December 2019
1st December SUNDAY

December 2019	
2nd December MONDAY	• VOC Starts at 12:27
3rd November TUESDAY	• The Moon enters Pisces at 07:10 • VOC Ends at 07:10
4th December WEDNESDAY	• The Moon enters its First Quarter at 06:58 in Pisces
5th December THURSDAY	• VOC Starts at 08:14 • The Moon enters Aries at 19:44 • VOC Ends at 19:44
6th December FRIDAY	
7th December	• VOC Starts at 15:01 • Mercury Leaves Rx Zone at 11:59 in Scorpio

SATURDAY	
8th December SUNDAY	• The Moon enters Taurus at 07:29 • VOC Ends at 07:29

December 2019	
9th December MONDAY	
10th December TUESDAY	• VOC Starts at 01:12 • The Moon enters Gemini at 16:46 • VOC Ends at 16:46
11th December WEDNESDAY	
12th December THURSDAY	• The **Full Moon** in Gemini at 05:12 • VOC Starts at 05:12 • The Moon enters Cancer at 23:32 • VOC Ends at 23:32 • Chiron leaves Retrograde
13th December FRIDAY	
14th December SATURDAY	• VOC Starts at 15:56
15th December SUNDAY	• The Moon enters Leo at 03:55 • VOC Ends at 03:55

December 2019	
16th December MONDAY	• VOC Starts at 22:09
17th December TUESDAY	• The Moon enters Virgo at 07:15 • VOC Ends at 07:15
18th December WEDNESDAY	• The Time of Osiris Begins
19th December THURSDAY	• The Moon enters its Last Quarter at 04:56 in Virgo • VOC Starts at 08:06 • The Moon enters Libra at 10:04 • The Time of Isis Begins
20th December FRIDAY	
21st December SATURDAY	• VOC Starts at 11:45 • The Moon enters Scorpio at 12:57 • VOC Ends at 12:57 • The Month of Sagittarius Ends • The Month of the Owl Ends
22nd December SUNDAY	• **Yule** at 04:49 (The Winter Solstice – Northern Hemisphere) • **Litha** at 04:49 (The Summer Solstice – Southern Hemisphere) • The Month of Capricorn Begins • The Month of the Goose Begins

December 2019	
23rd December MONDAY	• VOC Starts at 03:27 • The Moon enters Sagittarius at 16:54 • VOC Ends at 16:54 • The Month of the Falcon Ends • The Month of Elder Ends

24th December TUESDAY	• The Month of the Stag Begins • The Month of Birch Begins • Saturn Leaves Rx Zone at 40:34 in Capricorn • Christmas Eve
25th December WEDNESDAY	• VOC Starts at 11:18 • The Moon enters Capricorn at 21:45 • VOC Ends at 21:45 • Christmas Day
26th December THURSDAY	• The **New Moon** in Capricorn at 05:12 • An Annular Solar Eclipse at 05:17
27th December FRIDAY	• VOC Starts at 21:02
28th December SATURDAY	• The Moon enters Aquarius at 05:20 • VOC Ends at 05:20
29th December SUNDAY	• Vesta Leaves Retrograde

December 2019	
30th December MONDAY	• VOC Starts at 10:23 • The Moon enters Pisces at 15:41 • VOC Ends at 15:41
31st December TUESDAY	• The Time of Isis Ends

Thank you 2019

Section 3

Zodiac Calendars

The Zodiac are signs that represent characteristics in our lives, be it our behaviour, our relationships with others, our drive for success; so on and so forth. Different cultures use Animals, Trees and other natural entities. These are some of the most popular Zodiac calendars:

- Traditional Astrological Zodiac
- Native American Zodiac
- Celtic Animal Zodiac
- Celtic Tree Zodiac
- Chinese Zodiac
- Egyptian Zodiac
- Tibetan Zodiac
- Aztec Astrology

Traditional Astrological Zodiac

Sign	Dates	Representation
Aries	22nd March	The Ram

	to 19th April	
Taurus	20th April to 20th May	The Bull
Gemini	21st May to 20th June	The Twins
Cancer	21st June to 22nd July	The Crab
Leo	23rd July to 22nd August	The Lion
Virgo	23rd August to 22nd September	The Virgin
Libra	23rd September to 22nd October	The Scales
Scorpio	23rd October to 21st November	The Scorpion
Sagittarius	22nd November to 21st December	The Archer
Capricorn	22nd December to 19th January	The Sea-goat
Aquarius	20th January to 18th February	The Water Bearer
Pisces	19th February to 20th March	The Two Fishes

<u>Characteristics of the Signs</u>

Aries

Aries are the proverbial energiser bunny of the Zodiac signs; they have boundless energy and a real zest for life. Watching them can makes those around them feel tired. Aries will always get to the point, they do not walk on egg shells for anyone and they are not afraid to speak their mind. They have a very candid persona and careful planning before talking to an Aries could keep you away from uncomfortable and unpleasant conflicts. The Aries sign can't just sit back and watch they world they have to be a part of it.

Taurus

Taurus is associated with tremendous strength and well known for its steadfast, plodding along at a steady pace, but if someone they love is in need of protection they could out pace and out run an Olympic gold medallist. They are fierce, and won't back down until they have bested their opponent. Taurus is a sign that is dependable and predictable but that doesn't mean they can't step away from their predictability to do what needs to be done and it's their determination that wins out eventually. The Taurus signs aren't risk takers.

Gemini

Gemini is a butterfly that will flutter from one thing to another. They are seekers of knowledge but will flit from one subject to another. Gemini's have a similar characteristic when it comes to jobs, careers and relationships. They never delve too deeply and always get out before they get too far, and this can earn them a reputation of being shallow. Much like a Gemini being butterfly-like; they will gracefully move from one person to another, greeting them. Gemini's never stay in one place for too long. Gemini's are well spoken and resourceful.

Cancer

Cancer is sometimes hard on the outside but once you get to know them are kind hearted and sensitive. Their outer shell acts as a protective layer, a shield; to save their soft heart from pain and sorrow. Once you pass this shielded veneer they are charismatic, thoughtful and warm hearted. While you are getting to know the Cancer sign they will appear cold and distant which is actually contrary to their true nature. They are however adaptable and now how to ride the wave to come out of challenges with little to no harm. The Cancer sign is very emotional.

Leo

Leo is a good leader, they are the truest of humanitarians, they are often dedicated to protect and serve... at times the service is that of a carnal kind. Leo has great strength, power and a regal energy like its Lion counterpart. When a Leo uses their gifts for good they are almost saint-like, putting the needs of others before that of their own. However, if they choose to do the opposite they can be vindictive with their strength and power, denying those in need the help they are seeking. As a Leo they are driven to succeed and to be the best at it. They are the fore-runners, the leader of the Pride.

Virgo

A Virgo is incredibly strong, fierce and wholly independent pursing perfection. Virgo's are selective and very perceptive so it may seem like they are distant and prudish but they tend to see the intentions of others and decide whether or not they will share themselves. They can be the typical wallflower, but to the small groups they connect to they will happily share their hearts and spirits. One of the hardest things about being a Virgo is their dislike and distaste about messes. They are dedicated to organisation.

Libra

The Libra sign lives for beauty, harmony, balance and justice for all, however, the mind of Libra is always on the go and at times it can be nothing but fluff. Whether at home or in their work they seek for balance and harmony and if things are out of whack they are driven crazy. Keeping everything in balance take a lot of energy for a Libra, and they sometimes spread themselves a little too thin. They have a great sense of fun and a bright, clever mind even if they can't ever make up their mind.

Scorpio

Scorpio's are often described as mysterious and deadly and are known for their highly sexual charged. A Scorpio is driven by the giving and receiving of love; for them the form doesn't matter as long as they are able to share the highest vibrational emotion, love. A Scorpio can go from love and light to death and the macabre with the flick of a switch, so much so that it can catch others off guard. Scorpio's are creatures that are ever changing, evolving, growing and maturing. They have an amazingly loving side, but they also have a dark side to match.

Sagittarius

Sagittarius cannot sit still for long; they are the go-getters of the zodiac. They are enthusiastic and idealistic. If a Sagittarius sets their mind on something, their prey had better watch out and they will hit the target. Sagittarius people love a life that is full of adventure; they think big and follow through to act big. They know that life has much more to it than just work, and will dedicate much of their time to finding all that life has to offer. They are the globe trotters of the zodiac. Sagittarius people can find it hard to stay focused on what needs to be done.

Capricorn

Capricorns are ambitious; they are always reaching for their goals, setting them higher and higher. The height doesn't matter because they are sure-footed and always know where to step. Those born under Capricorn are born with an innate sense of wisdom but sometimes they can be intimidating. Capricorns are on an eternal search for self-worth but it is the one thing that always eludes them. Capricorns are consistent, they do not gamble. They are the planners and they follow the plan to the letter, never taking a gamble. Capricorns are quiet signs, choosing their strategy over fluffy or pointless words.

Aquarius

People born under the sign of Aquarius are the forward thinkers, they are the dreamers and they are the rebels that lead causes they are passionate about. They are friendly, smart and loyal who make friends easily; but for some they are trodden all over by unscrupulous people who have no care for the friendly Aquarius. They are eccentric, eclectic and very independent. They are driven by their emotions but sometimes their sense of freedom comes at a cost. Their eccentricity and desire to stay to themselves can make them appear aloof to those who don't know them.

Pisces

The Pisces sign is delicate and sensitive being that strive to show the world what it means to love unconditionally. When they are set on making the world a better place they will experience a rollercoaster but they will always ride the waves and stay the course. The major influence in the life of a Pisces is the Moon so it's not surprising that they have mood swings that will wax and wane like the Moon. People born in Pisces will try to save the world and be everything to everyone, but they often neglect themselves. They are transformative.

Native American Zodiac

Sign	Dates
Otter	20th January to 18th February
Wolf	19th February to 20th March
Falcon	21st March to 19th April
Beaver	20th April to 20th May
Deer	21st May to 20th June
Woodpecker	21st June to 21st July
Salmon	22nd July 21st August
Bear	22nd August to 21st September
Raven	22nd September to 22nd October
Snake	23rd October to 22nd November
Owl	23rd November to 21st December

| Goose | 22nd December to 19th January |

<u>Characteristics of the Signs</u>

Otter

The Otter is quirky and a little bit unorthodox; they are perceived as unconventional and often are the first choice to get things done, but this is often a mistake because they have method in their madness and these methods tend to actually get the job done. They do have an odd outlook on life but they have a brilliant mind and are extremely imaginative which can give them an edge. Otters are very perceptive and rely on their intuition to make decisions. Otters make great friends as they are nurturing, sympathetic, attentive, loyal and honest beings.

Wolf

The Wolf is extremely emotional and passionate; they are the lover of the Native American Zodiac, whether it is metaphorical, philosophical or literal. The Wolf understands the power that love can bring to your life and is capable is sharing their own special kind of love. The Wolf is a contradiction because as much as they are loving, caring and compassionate they can be distant when they crave freedom and independence. The Wolf is passionate, affectionate and generous; however they can become obsessive and impractical at times.

Falcon

The Falcon is a natural born leader and others trust their sense of judgement, especially if you

are in a sticky situation. They don't waste their
time, they prefer to take the initiative to "strike
while the iron is hot" doing what has to be done
when it has to be done. Falcons can be a little
arrogant but they tend to be right so a little bit of
big-headedness is understood. Given the right
environment a Falcon will sour but left to its own
devices they can become vain, impatient and rude.

Beaver

The Beaver is adaptable when it comes to
challenging situations. The Beaver is all
business and works hard to get the job done
quickly and efficiently. When they get going
the Beaver is a force to be reckoned with.
They have a razor-sharp mind and very quick
witted and tend to lean toward the "my way or
the highway" mentality. Even though the
Beaver is right most of the time this mind-set
can get them in sticky situations when they
lack the tact to not rub people the wrong way.
The Beaver is generous, nurturing and helpful
as well as cunning and a great strategist.

Deer (or Stag)

The Deer is the inspiration, the muse and a
true conversationalist. They are quick witted,
lively and can pull a laugh out of anyone;
their lively aura makes them a great guest at
parties because they are great talkers mixed
with fantastic intelligence making them able
to talk to anyone and everyone. The Deer is
always aware of their surroundings. They can
tailor themselves to every situation. When the
Deer is in a positive environment the energy if

the Deer is magnified and their sparkly personality will really shine, their liveliness inspiring others too.

Woodpecker

The Woodpecker is the most nurturing of the Native American Zodiac. They are exceptional listeners that always have understanding for others. Woodpeckers are always great to have in your corner as they will loyally support others. The Woodpeckers make great friends, partners and parents because they have a deep sense of empathy and nurturing. Those born in the sign of the Woodpecker are resourceful; they are frugal and make everything stretch a little further. The woodpecker is devoted and very romantic when they are in a safe and happy environment.

Salmon

The Salmon is a very creative sign. They are focused with an energy that is palpable. Their energy and enthusiasm infects those around them and their confidence is inspiring. It is easy to get caught up in their ideas even if they seem like the most hare-brained scheme ever conceived. The Salmon is generous and intelligent and has a strong need to have a goal to work towards. They are sensitive, sensual and giving and have no shortage of friends and supporters.

Bear

The Bear is the practical, level-headed and methodical; these qualities make the Bear the best business partner. The Bear is the steady-hand or the voice of reason in most situations. The Bear has a big heart making them very generous, but they are shy and live modestly. The Bear is very patient and will wait until the time is exactly right, and this has allowed them to become great teachers and mentors. The Bear is a lover of a sign, but they are strong and protective.

Raven

The Raven is the entrepreneur, the charmer and enthusiastic, and all of this comes as naturally as breathing. They are easy going yet idealistic and diplomatic, they aren't always the most conventional but this is what makes the Raven so endearing. The Raven can be soft-spoken, shy and patient. Those who are born under the Raven sign can create an intuitive, nurturing and harmonious space where they can be themselves. The Raven's charm can sometimes go bad and turn to manipulation – it is a fine line that the Raven walks.

Snake

Many of the Native American Shamans are born under the sign of the Snake because they have a natural affinity for all forms of

spirituality which makes them ideal to be
healers and leaders. The Snake is respected
for their healing characteristics. The nature of
the Snake may seem to always be out of reach
or intangible which has lead them to be seen
as mysterious; they have also been feared as
much as they have been fawned over. The
Snake can be secretive and seem to be on the
'dark side' but they are actually very loving,
caring and passionate once you break though
their air of mystery.

Owl

The Owl is as changeable as the winds and
can be difficult to pin them down on one place
for any length of time. The Owl is easy-going,
warm and a friend to everyone. They take on
life at break-neck speed and give every
adventure their all. Sometimes the Owl can be
reckless or careless because they forget that
not everyone sees life the same way they do.
The Owl makes great teachers, artists and
mentors and with their innate creativity they
excel at these. Their flexibility means they can
handle different tasks with enthusiasm. When
an Owl is left to their down thing they can be
a little excessive.

Goose

The Goose is the one to go to if you have
something that needs to get done because
they will doggedly work to get it done. The

Goose sets itself goals and their ambitious
nature means they will attain them.
Sometimes they can be their own enemies by
tripping themselves on their ambition. The
Goose is a very competitive which drives them
to win, which is great for competitive sports.
The Goose always excels at whatever they set
their mind to. The Goose can be supportive,
passionate and sensual with the right people.

Celtic Animal Zodiac

Sign	Dates
Cat	21st January to 17th February
Snake	18th February to 17th March
Fox	18th March to 14th April
Cow	15th April to 12th May
Seahorse	13th May to 9th June
Wren	10th June to 7th July
Horse	8th July to 4th August
Fish	5th August to 1st September
Swan	2nd September to 29th September
Butterfly	30th September to 27th October
Wolf	28th October to 24th November
Falcon	25th November to 23rd December
Stag	24th December to 20th January

Characteristics of the Signs

Cat

The Cat doesn't matter if they are on the
fringe, in fact this is the perfect for them
because they can sit and observe everything

that is going on. It is common knowledge that cats have a sixth sense; which allow them to perceive underlying emotions and motivations of other people. The Cat has the ability to see things in a different light from everyone else and don't fear going somewhere new. The time spent on the side lines allows them to pick up on the details of situations that others miss by charging in.

Adder (Snake)

The Adder is very persuasive; they are natural communicators and are able to talk to almost everyone. They are also naturally very curious and always studying, always wanting to know more. The Adder is very astute and constantly watching the interactions of people surrounding them, they can be amazing at rallying others to a cause. The Adder can be very spontaneous and unpredictable; and at times they even question their own motives but they always have a reason. They can be abrasive and can be confrontational if they are pushed too far. Especially when defending their nest.

Fox

The Fox is cunning, sly and intelligent so if you need someone to go on fantastic adventures with you, the Fox is the one. Their ability to work a room means that if you find yourself in a sticky spot they Fox can get you out, in fact, no one is better at it. The Fox is an exceptionally strong spirit that cannot be manipulated or dominated by anyone; their sly nature wouldn't let them. Foxes are courageous, loyal and very affectionate, so if you make it into the Fox's inner circle you will see a very different side to them. They are the friend for life

Cow (Bull)

The Cow is as solid as a rock, they have broad shoulders and these characteristics carry over into the Celtic Animal Zodiac too. The Cow is strong, stable and very caring; however when it comes to protecting the ones they love they are an unmovable, stubborn force that will not budge. The Cow is a very trustworthy sign, and they dislike others lying to them. The Cow has a strong intuition of knowing when someone is lying to them. They see the bigger picture, often seeing what is going on before anyone else.

Seahorse

The Seahorse is flexible, adaptable and very resourceful. Those born under the sign of the Seahorse may not be the biggest or the strongest; but to them that doesn't matter their quick-mind and resourcefulness allow them to adapt to every situation. They are the ultimate finder of loopholes; this makes them great at working with complex situations such as finance or the law. Their adaptability makes these areas perfect for the Seahorse.

The seahorse is wise, affectionate and loving. They are well loved and respected.

Wren

The Wren has a very sunny and warm disposition which is rarely dimmed. The Wren has a strong moral code which includes honour, integrity and responsibility but these don't impact their happy vibrations. They love to be the one cheering people up; this aside they are steadfast friends that won't abandon their friends or family if they are in the midst of a bad situation. Wrens are naturally caring and devoted making them great caregivers but normally the Wren will work alone. The hardest things for a Wren are finding a sense of balance as they feel the weight of responsibility.

Horse

The Horse is strong and proud, powerful and competitive; they tend to charge into every situation – sometimes with all "guns blazing". Horses are very talented and when they like to show off, they have the ability to back it up. Naturally the Horse is gregarious and boisterous and this helps them if they are in the business world. They are the powerful go-getters. The Horse is very good at navigating the path forward and will work well as a leader or as a member of a team, as long as they are doing something. Horses are headstrong and won't back down if difficult times roll around.

Fish (Salmon)

The Fish tend to be artistic in nature and will find their inspiration after they have delved deep into themselves. They have a very unique view of the world and are relatively introverted. Their intuition isn't as noticeable as other signs, but it is there, sitting quietly in the background. The Fish have a great gift for the arts, poetry or writing. They are sometimes seemed as inspiration when they finally join the real world after spending time in their own inner world.

Swan

The Swan will have reached their place and status on life through spiritual growth and transformation. They are eloquent, refined and pride themselves on their keen eye for beauty and their taste. The Swan can sometimes come across as detached but this is actually far from the truth, they are simply very composed and have a strong sense of honour and stick to a code of conduct. They are passionate and care about all of the details; they are just reserved about their passions.

Butterfly

The Butterfly is the most social of the Celtic Animals Signs. They are gentle, kind and caring souls. They love to flit from place to place and hate to be stood in one place for too long. They are the dreamers; they always know the best ways to cheer people up. Their natural empathy means that they are easy to befriend, they are the undyingly loyal and will do everything they can to make sure they make your day. They are gentle. They are freedom seekers.

Wolf

The Wolf is an inherently social animal that runs with a pack, and the 'lone wolf' is not always the case. They are the exception not the rule. People born under the sign of the Wolf can appear to be anti-social, this can be because they don't feel like they it with you. However; if a Wolf accepts you into their pack/inner circle they will be gracious, social, kind, fearless and protective. They are the ones who can push you to reach your goals or get to the finish line. They are uncompromising with their loyalty and can be stubborn; can be a pain in the butt with their stubborn tendencies.

Falcon (Hawk)

The Falcon is a keen-sighted, they spot their prey for a distance and when the time is right they will swoop in with a single-minded focus. If nothing catches their eye they will fly from place to place until something grabs their attention. They are open to new ideas, thoughts and philosophies but no matter where they go, they follow a set moral compass and will rarely, if ever falter. The Falcon are fans of debates and will happily spend hours sharing ideas and debating, but they can be hard to persuade because of their strong internal compass.

Stag (Deer)

The Stag is a powerful symbol in Celtic beliefs as a sign in nobility, royalty and honesty. They are hard working, and it's this; that allows the Stag to succeed as many times as they do. When they believe in something they cannot be deterred from achieving their goal.

Celtic Tree Zodiac

Sign	Dates
Rowan	21st January to 7th February
Ash	8th February to 17th February
Alder	18th March to 14th April
Willow	15th April to 12th May
Hawthorn	13th May to 16th June
Oak	10th June to 7th July
Holly	8th July to 4th August
Hazel	5th August to 1st September
Vine	2nd September to 29th

	September
Ivy	30th September to 27th October
Reed	28th October to 24th November
Elder	25th November to 23rd December
Birch	24th December to 20th January

Characteristics of the Signs

Rowan

Rowan is the most philosophical of all of the Celtic Tree Signs; and this means they sometimes can be aloof, feeling that no one really understands them. The Rowan signs are often seen as visionaries and highly creative thoughts. Those born under the Rowan sign are full of energy and passion. They are very devoted to whatever they are doing, they are also very persuasive.

Ash

The Ash sign are the free thinkers. They possess a vivid imaginations and incredible powers of intuition. Those born under the Ash sign tend to follow creative career paths or have artistic hobbies. They are drawn to the spiritual, the artistic and the creative. For those born under the Ash sign their inner world is always changing forms, they are as changing as the winds. At times they see the world with crystal clear clarity, at other times they are moody, withdrawn and sullen.

Alder

The Alder sign is all about forging a path ahead, they have a magical way with words which means they can easily and quickly gain followers for a cause. They are charming, charismatic and confident. They are sure of themselves and the cause they fight for, having faith they that will reach any goal that is set for them, or set by them. Those born under the sign of Alder cannot tolerate those who waste their time. They would rather move on and focus their energy elsewhere.

Willow

The Willow sign tends to be highly intuitive and very creative; they often possess a higher range of intelligence. They understand the different cycles in life and instinctively know that everything in life teaches you something. They are able to take the lessons of the past and apply them effortlessly to future situations. The Willow sign has a lot in common with the Moon and how it changes constantly.

Hawthorn

The Hawthorn sign isn't always as they first appear. They are full of an unquenchable curiosity and they are able to adapt to anything that life throws at them, usually because their inner world isn't always what the exterior world sees. They are shape shifters and will test the old saying "never judge a book by its cover" because you never know which book you are going to get with the Hawthorn.

Oak

The Oak is the stabilising force of the Celtic Tree Zodiac. Those born under the sign of Oak were said to possess an unworldly gift of strength. They are the protectors of the weak, defenders of the defenceless and they will give a voice to those who have none. They are always kind, gentle and generous. The Oak sign has a deep respect for their ancestry and their history and it's this love that leads some of them to become teacher or social workers.

Holly

The Holly sign is the most noble of the Celtic Tree Signs and have the skills of a natural born leader. They are able to adapt to challenges and easily rise through the ranks, gaining power and status. They are able to tackle the hardest or most complex tasks and they do so with integrity and tact. Those born under the sign of Holly love to have an active lifestyle because otherwise they become complacent and lazy. They are ambitious but they have what is needed to back it up.

Hazel

The Hazel sign is highly intelligent and excels
in the classroom. Academically they are the
bees-knees because knowledge comes easy to
them. They have the ability to recall and
recite information that they have learned
previously, and at times with near perfection.
Sometimes the Hazel can appear as a know it
all, but they can't help being smart, that is
just how they were born.

Vine

Another shape-shifter in the Celtic Tree
Zodiac is the Vine, and they are
unpredictable, indecisive and will often
contradict themselves. They always are the
good and the bad in equal measure because
they are born under the influence of the
equinox. This makes it hard for them to pick
a side, making them chose the impartial path.
The Vine has a weak spot for guilty pleasure
and that is luxury and refinement – they like
the better things in life.

Ivy

Ivy is the sign that will overcome any
hardship and survive through any situation.
They are the ultimate survivor of the Celtic
Tree Zodiac. The Ivy sign are very loyal and

compassionate. Sometimes life can be hard on them but they endure everything that the Universe throws their way with grace and integrity. They are deeply spiritual and their faith is deeply rooted in the world of the spiritual. They are calm and softly spoken, which adds to their endearment.

Reed

The Reed sign is the secret keeper of the Celtic Tree Signs. They love to dig up secrets and discover the truth and the real meaning behind things. Those born under the Reed love a good story, they love a good mystery too; this means that the Reed is perfect for a detective, journalist or even an archaeologist. They have the ability to look at something and see it for what it truly is, getting right to the core of everything. Even though the Reed can be a little manipulative it can also have a deep sense of honour and a strong moral code.

Elder

The Elder sign is the free spirit, they love to be able to move from place to place and often seem like they are untamed or wild, and that is just how they like it. They love adventure and discovering all that life has to offer. Sometimes it seems like they are only living in the fast lane and missing life, but they are extremely thoughtful and very considerate. They are often the most helpful sign. Elder is

often very misunderstood and can be judged
harshly.

Birch

The Birch tend to have a fresh and sometimes
unusual outlook on life, but they always full
of ambition, energy and zest for life. They are
very driven, striving for more and more,
pushing them-selves further to get to new
horizons, reaching higher. People born under
the Birch can be quite gruff but they are
always tolerant of people and will lead others
with a kind heart. They are the sunshine in
the room and can quickly charm even the
gloomiest of people.

Chinese Zodiac

2019 is the Year of the Boar/Pig

Animal	Years
Rat	1948, 1960, 1972, 1984, 1996, 2008, 2020
Ox	1949, 1961, 1973, 1985, 1997, 2009, 2021
Tiger	1950, 1962, 1974, 1986, 1998 2010, 2022
Rabbit	1951, 1963, 1975, 1987, 1999, 2011, 2023
Dragon	1952, 1964, 1976, 1988, 2000, 2012, 2024
Snake	1953, 1965,1977, 1989, 2001, 2013, 2025

Horse	1954, 1966, 1978, 1990, 2002, 2014, 2026
Sheep	1955, 1967, 1979, 1991, 2003, 2015, 2026
Monkey	1956, 1968, 1980, 1992, 2004, 2016, 2027
Rooster	1957, 1969, 1981, 1993, 2005, 2017, 2029
Dog	1958, 1970, 1982, 1994, 2006, 2018, 2030.
Pig/Boar	1947, 1959, 1971, 1983, 1995, 2007, **2019**

Characteristics of the Signs

Rat

Those born under the sign of the Rat are instinctive, acute and alert in nature which will make then great business men and women, very savvy. They can always react properly before the worst of circumstances take place. Those born under the sign of the Rat are sophisticated and popular in social interactions; they are adaptable, and are popular with others

- Strengths of the Rat – Adaptable, Smart, Cautious, Acute, Alert, Positive, Flexible, Out-going and Cheerful
- Weaknesses of the Rat – Timid, Unstable, Stubborn, Picky, lack of Persistence and Procrastination

Ox

Those born under the sign of the Ox are persistent, simple, honest and very straight forward. They are leaders with a strong faith and a strong devotion to their work and career. They contemplate all avenues before taking action, they aren't easily affected by their surroundings; they follow their own concepts and ability. Those born under the sign of the Ox can lack wit while speaking and socialising so can come across as very quiet, stubborn or stuck in their ways.

- Strengths of the Ox – Honest, Industrious, Patient, Hard-working, Cautious, Level-headed, Strong-willed and Persistent.
- Weaknesses of the Ox – Obstinate, Inarticulate, Prudish and Distant.

Tiger

Those born under the sign of the Tiger are powerful, independent, confident and very brave. They have a strong sense of adventure, to travel. They are frank people and win the trust of others easily. Those born under the sign of the Tiger will go through many hardships but once the trials are over they will often enjoy a bright and prosperous life. They may be dogmatic and live showing off when the accomplish something.

- Strengths of the Tiger – Tolerant, Loyal, Valiant, Courageous, Trustworthy, Intelligent, and Virtuous.
- Weaknesses of the Tiger – Arrogant, Short-tempered, Hasty, Traitorous.

Rabbit

Those born under the sign of the Rabbit usually impress others with their tenderness, grace and sensitivity. They are very romantic in relationships, having a high demand on the quality of their life. Those born under the sign of the Rabbit will do anything to avoid arguing and conflict with others, and have a capability of converting enemies into friends. They are homebodies and very hospitable. They don't get angry easily but they do like to hesitate which means they miss many opportunities and chances.

- Strengths of the Rabbit – Gentle, Sensitive, Compassionate, Amiable, Modest and Merciful.
- Weaknesses of the Rabbit – Amorous, Hesitant, Stubborn, Timid and Conservative.

Dragon

Those born under the sign of the Dragon are usually lively, intellectual and quite excitable. They have a very clear sense of right and wrong. They are also very upright and forthright people. However people born under the sign of the Dragon can be a little arrogant and impatient. They have a strong aversion to hypocrisy, gossip and slander; they aren't afraid of difficulties. They hate to be used or controlled by others.

- Strengths of the Dragon – Decisive, Inspiring, Sensitive, Magnanimous, Ambitious and Romantic.
- Weaknesses of the Dragon – Eccentric, Tactless, Fiery, Intolerant and Unrealistic.

Snake

Those born under the sign of the Snake are misunderstood; they are seen as cunning and sly but they're wise and have great sense of wit. They are sensitive people with a fantastic sense of humour and many of them are gifted in literature and the arts. Those born under the sign of the Snake are naturally suspicious which can lead to paranoia.

- Strengths of the Snake – Soft-spoken, Humorous, Smart, Sympathetic, Determined and Passionate.
- Weaknesses of the Snake – Jealous, Suspicious, Sly, Fickle, and Nonchalant.

Horse

Those born under the sign of the Horse appear to be dynamic, zealous and generous. They have many shining qualities but they need to face their weaknesses. They have nice personalities which means they make friends easily. They don't give up when facing difficulties but their frank nature can lead them to letting secrets slip out easily, though unintentional.

- Strengths of the Horse – Warm-hearted, Upright, Easy-going, Independence, and Endurance.
- Weaknesses of the Horse – Spending – they will need to have financial affluence to support their lifestyle, Lack of Persistence.

Sheep

Those born under the sign of the Sheep are tender, polite, clever and kind-hearted. They have a special kind of sensitivity which means they have a special fondness toward having a quiet life. They are wise, gentle and extremely compassionate; they cope with their business cautiously and try hard to be economical in their day to day life. Those born under the sign of the Sheep are willing to take care of others. They can be hesitant and pessimistic.

- Strengths of the Sheep – gentle, Soft-hearted, Considerate, Attractive, Hardworking, Persistent, and Thrifty.
- Weaknesses of the Sheep -Indecisive, Timid, Vain, Moody, Pessimistic and Weak-willed.

Monkey

Those born under the sign of the Monkey are smart, clever and intelligent, especially when it comes to their career and finances. They are very lively, flexible and quick-witted people. They are gentle and honest which help them to create an everlasting love life. Those born under the sign of the Monkey have very enviable qualities they do have short comings, they tend to look down on others and have a temper.

- Strengths of the Monkey – Enthusiastic, Self-assured, Sociable, and Innovative.
- Weaknesses of the Monkey – jealous, Suspicious, Cunning, Selfish and Arrogant.

Rooster

Those born under the sign of the Rooster have many fantastic qualities such as honest, bright and they are excellent communicators. They're born with a great facial bone structure making them pretty and handsome. They are very self-reliant and will seldom rely on others for anything. Those born under the sign of the Rooster may be enthusiastic about something one moment and impassive or bored the next moment. They need to have enough faith and patience to stick to one thing.

- Strengths of the Rooster – Independent, Capable, Warm-hearted, Self-respect, and Quick-minded.

- Weaknesses of the Rooster – Impatient, critical, Selfish, Eccentric and Narrow-minded.

Dog

Those born under the sign of the Dog are usually very independent, sincere, loyal and extremely decisive. They're unafraid of difficulties in their day to day life. Those born under the sign of the Dog have very harmonious relationships in every area of their lives.

- Strengths of the Dog – Valiant, Loyal, Responsible, Clever, Courageous, and Lively.
- Weaknesses of the Dog – Sensitive, Conservative, Stubborn and Emotional.

Pig

Those born under the sign of the Pig are considerate, responsible, independent and optimistic. They always show mercy to other people's mistakes, their generosity and this mercy will help them to create positive interpersonal relationships. Those born under the sign of the Pig can be lazy and resist taking action. They have pure hearts which could lead to having a broken heart.

- Strengths of the Pig – Warm-hearted, Good-tempered, Loyal, Honest and Gentle.

- Weaknesses of the Pig – Naive, Gullible, Sluggish and Short-tempered.

Tibetan Zodiac

The Tibetan Astrology system has drawn a lot of inspiration from Buddhism and based on the year you were born much like the Chinese Zodiac.

2019 is the sign of the Copper Bracelet

Cobra

Years of the Cobra – 1893, 1905, 1917, 1929, 1941, 1953, 1965, 1977, 1989, 2001, 2013.

Those born under the sign of the Cobra are very seductive and have a certain kind of magnetism and tend to find a lot of luck in love. They are sexual, passionate and deeply sensual. Those born under the sign of the Cobra can brighten up the room and people love to be in their presence.

Fire Guardian

Years of the Fire Guardian – 1894, 1906, 1918, 1930, 1942, 1954, 1966, 1978, 1990, 2002, 2014.

Those born under the sign of the Fire Guardian are fiercely protective and always at hand to help those lost and wayward souls. They bring warmth and comfort to those around them, which helps people suffering from psychological trauma feel safe. Those born under the sign of the Fire Guardian bring light where darkness dwells.

Crystalline Water Spring

Years of the Crystalline Water Spring – 1895,
1907, 1919, 1931, 1943, 1955, 1967, 1979, 1991,
2003, 2015.

Those born under the sign of the Crystalline Water
Spring have a very purifying energy. Their energy
makes people want to dive in and just bask there
in their energy. Those born under the sign of the
Crystalline Water Spring are extremely loyal to
those they love; and are calm and serene. They
have a deep tenderness and affection.

Jade Stele

Years of the Jade Stele – 1896, 1908, 1920, 1932,
1944, 1956, 1968, 1980, 1992, 2004, 2016.

Those born under the sign of the Jade Stele are
'inclusive'; they prefer to be secretive, which
makes them hard to understand and difficult to
connect with. Those born under the sign of the
Jade Stele have a gift with words, they can
transform a simple breath into words, giving
language a magical tone, or they can create a
meditative flow with a delightful silence.

Metal Gong

Years of the Metal Gong – 1897, 1909, 1921,
1933, 1945, 1957, 1969, 1981, 1993, 2005 2017.

Those born under the sign of the Metal Gong are
extremely honest people who tend to be deep in
thought. They always move at their own pace and
find great joy when they are able to overcome a
challenge. Those born under the sign of the Metal
Gong take on any challenge and obstacles that are
sent in their path and find immense satisfaction

once they find a way through anything set before them.

Lake Turtle

Those born under the sign of the Lake Turtle are extremely honest and have an considerable amount of sincerity. From time to time they need to have a little shake in order to stop them from procrastinating. Those born under the sign of the Lake Turtle sometimes have difficulties moving forward so need egging on from time to time.

Copper Bracelet

Those born under the sign of the Copper Bracelet are the most sensual of the Tibetan zodiac; they seek the world for sensual relationships. They are full of love and affection that they wish to share with others. Those under the sign of the Copper Bracelet need to have a life filled with carnal pleasure to feel good and fulfilled.

Black Buffalo

Those born under the sign of the Black Buffalo can set their gaze on something and they will go for it with all of their might. Those born under the

sign of the Black Buffalo don't beat about the
bush; they always go where their hearts lead
them, even if it means they will know pain in the
future.

New Moon

Those born under the sign of the New Moon live in
a dream world of their own making. They are
sweet, poetic and very romantic. Those born under
the sign of the New Moon have a passive nature
and will easily let themselves get swept away by
their intense emotions; and sometimes they need
someone to act as a tether.

Exalted Sun

Those born under of the sign of the Exalted Sun is
brimming with energy even though they are
humble they are quite talented. Those born under
the sign of the Exalted Sun make fantastic
companions who will help and push people to
excel and reach the height of their true potential.

Monk and Monkey

Those born under the sign of the Monk and
Monkey possess a certain detachment of which is

appropriate for a crone or sage. They are aware that everything is invariable and never lasts. Those born under the sign of the Monk and Monkey are compassionate even though it may come across as cold or distant.

Stag Beetle

Years of the Stag Beetle – 1904, 1916, 1928, 1940, 1952, 1964, 1976, 1988, 2000, 2012, 2024.

Those born under the sign of the Stag Beetle are bewitching and have an exquisite character. They sometimes suffer because of the deep sensitivity. Those born under the sign of the Stag Beetle are able to easily seduce others and able to take shelter and comfort in their vivid dreams when things start to take a bad turn.

Aztec Astrology

Aztec Astrology is more complex than other Astrology and Zodiac systems because the twenty divinities of the Aztec pantheon hold influence over the fates on man; each of these divinities influences a single month. Time is based on a cycle that alternates with the seasons – each day sign lasts around 24 hours and tends to be influenced by a number and a colour.

You can work out your Aztec sign by using the below instructions.

1) Select the number that matches the year you were born.

1900 – 17	1920 – 2	1940 – 7	1960 – 12
1901 – 3	1921 – 8	1941 – 13	1961 – 18
1902 – 8	1922 – 13	1942 – 18	1962 – 3
1903 – 13	1923 – 18	1943 – 3	1963 – 8
1904 – 18	1924 – 3	1944 – 8	1964 – 13
1905 – 4	1925 – 9	1945 – 14	1965 – 19
1906 – 9	1926 – 14	1946 – 19	1966 – 4
1907 – 14	1927 – 19	1947 – 4	1967 – 9
1908 – 19	1928 – 4	1948 – 9	1968 – 14
1909 – 9	1929 – 10	1949 – 15	1969 – 20
1910 – 10	1930 – 15	1950 – 20	1970 – 5
1911 – 15	1931 – 20	1951 – 5	1971 – 10
1912 – 20	1932- 5	1952 – 10	1972 – 15
1913 – 6	1933 – 11	1953 – 16	1973 – 1
1914 – 11	1934 – 16	1954 – 1	1974 – 6
1915 – 16	1935 -1	1955 – 6	1975 – 11
1916 – 1	1936 – 6	1956 – 11	1976 – 16
1917 – 7	1937 – 12	1957 – 7	1977 – 2
1918 – 12	1938 – 17	1958 – 2	1978 – 7
1919 - 17	1939 – 2	1959 – 7	1979 – 12

1980 – 17	2000 – 2
1981 – 3	2001 – 8
1982 – 8	2002 – 13
1983 – 13	2003 – 18
1984 – 18	2004 – 3
1985 – 4	2005 – 9
1986 – 9	2006 – 14
1987 – 14	2007 – 19
1988 – 19	2008 – 4
1989 – 5	2009 -10
1990 – 10	2010 – 15
1991 – 15	2011 – 20
1992 – 20	2012 – 5
1993 – 6	2013 – 11
1994 – 11	2014 – 16
1995 – 16	2015 – 1
1996 – 1	2016 – 6
1997 – 7	2017 – 12
1998 – 12	2018 – 12
1999 – 17	2019 – 2

2) Add your number from above with the number that corresponds to the month you were born.

January – 19	July – 0
February – 10	August – 11
March – 18	September – 2
April – 9	October – 12
May - 19	November – 3
June – 10	December – 13

3) Add these numbers to the day of the month you were born.

<table>
<tr><td>If you were born on the 7th, you would use the number 7</td></tr>
</table>

| If you were born on the 7th, you would use the number 7 |
| If you were born on the 29th of February you will need to add 1 to your overall total |

4) The number you should have obtained should be between 1 and 20; if not, divide the total by 20.

EXAMPLE

1) I was born in 1987 which means my number is **14**

2) I was born in February which means my number is **10**

3) I was born on the 20th which means my number is **20**

| 14 |
| + |
| 10 |
| + |
| 20 |
| = 44 |
| / by 20 |
| = 2.2 |

Only take the number BEFORE the decimal.

My number is

Characteristics of the Signs

1) Cayman or Crocodile – CIPACTI

Bears the number 1; and the colour light green. Those born under the sign of the Cayman/Crocodile carry a wealth of knowledge and wisdom; they have a very logical mind always looking for logic in situations. Those born under the sign of the Cayman/Crocodile are strong willed and fantastic organisers, they ha deep level of understanding in many different areas. The planet Venus is associated with this sign and its divine force is Tonacatecuhtli.

2) *Wind – EHECALT*

Bears the number 2. Those born under the sign of Wind have a talent for knowing how to overcome obstacles; when a storm rolls in those born under the sign of Wind always manage to calm themselves in the end. Those born under the sign of Wind are very flexible and as a result very agile with their time and abilities; however, they have a very strong moral compass. The planet Venus is associated with this sign and it's divine force is Quetzalcoatl

3) *House – CALLI*

Bears the number 3 and the colour dark green. Those born under the sign of the House are very welcoming and generous; they like to be around other people and will find a sense of complete balance with their soul mate. Those born under the sign of the House are rarely found on their own, finding their place among family and friends. They always find a routine that works for them. The planet Saturn is associated with this sign and its divine force is Tepeyolohti.

4) Lizard – CUETZPALLIN

Bears the number 4. Those born under the sign of
the Lizard are very lively; they have a vivacity that
is unique to them. Those born under the sign of
the Lizard can handle any situation the universe
places in their path and are very resilient to-boot.
When they are faced with obstacles they are
prudent, looking at every possibility before taking
action. The planet Saturn is associated with this
sign and its divine force is Huehuecoyotl.

5) Snake – COATL

Bears the number 5 and the colour orange. Those
born under the sign of the Snake are adventurous
and have quite a strong spontaneous streak. They
can act without thinking from time to time. Those
born under the sign of the Snake can take people
by surprise with their actions and reactions. To
the Aztec people the Snake symbolises the
reconciliation between heaven and earth. The
Snake can also be a sign that's a little lazy. The
planet Saturn is associated with this sign and its
divine force is Chalchicitlicue.

6) Death – MIQUIZTLI

Bears the number 6 and is the colour
purple. Those born under the sign of Death
are very introverted; they feel like they
aren't able to be themselves around other
people. Those born under the sign of Death
tend to prefer their own company, being
satisfied with solitary activities. The Moon
is represents this sign and its divine forces
are Tecciztecatl and Meztli.

7) Stag/Deer – MAZATL

Bears the number 7. Those born under the sign of the Stag/Deer are shy and reserved, and are often dreamers. They are tenacious people, always ready to hold fast to what they believe to be important. Those born under the sig of the Stag/Deer are very sociable, and like to be around their friends and family. The Moon is associated with this sign and its divine force is Tlaloc.

8) Rabbit – TOCHTLI

Bears the number 8 and the colour Indigo. Those born under the sign of the Rabbit enjoy all of life's pleasures to the fullest. They are quite timid and delicate, and will do whatever they have to, to avoid any kind of conflict. Those born under the sign of the Rabbit are remarkably hard working, but they are fantastic company too, even when they are working. They always have a smile for people. The Moon is associated with this sign, and its divine force is Mayohuel.

9) Water – ATL

Bears the number 9. Those born under the sign of Water are born worriers, they can be crippled with fear and instability they find hard to find their way out of the darkness; this can be connected to their very sensitive nature; which can also help others find their way out of their darkness. The planet Mars is associated with this sign and its divine force is Xiuhtecuhtli.

10)   Dog – ITZCUINTLI

Bears the number 10. Those born under the sign of the Dog are exceedingly generous people and will do whatever they can to help others out; they like to feel they are being useful. They are truly intuitive and incredibly brave; yet shy at the same time. The planet Mars is associated with this sign and its divine force is Mictlantecuhtli.

11)   Monkey – OZOMTLI

Bears the number 11 and the colour golden yellow. Those born under the sign of the Monkey are terribly charming and rather modest and they have the ability to adapt to changing situations. Those born under the sign of the Monkey have something seductive about them, and are blessed with natural beauty; along with this beauty they are pleasant. The Monkey is an important sign for the Aztec, as a Monkey gave them fire in an act of great compassion. The planet Mars is associated with this sign, and its divine force is Xochipilli.

12)   Grass – MALINALLI

Bears the number 12. Those born under the sign of Grass are very uncommonly complex; they can be positive and upbeat one moment and the next they can be fighting off very negative thoughts or feelings which can lead to negative actions. They often find themselves in the midst of trials, which they must overcome. Those born under the sign of Grass are both sensitive and resilient. The planet Jupiter

is associated with this sign and its divine
force is Patecatl.

13)   Reed – ACATL

Bears the number 13. Those born under
the sign of the Reed love life and are full of
optimism; they believe there can be
paradise on earth. They enjoy all of the
pleasures and delights that life has to offer;
especially the simple things in life. Those
born under the sign of the Reed are happy
and content with what they have in life,
and are happy with the life they lead. The
planet Jupiter is associated with this sign
and its divine forces are Tezcatlipoca and
Itzlacoliuhqui.

14)   Jaguar – OCELOTL

Bears the number 14 and its associated
colour is Black. Those born under the sign
of the Jaguar have a great strength of
character, but can easily become
aggressive especially if they get carried
away. Those born under the sign of the
Jaguar have wandering eyes and may be
unfaithful in their relationships. The planet
Jupiter is associated with this sign and its
divine force is Tlazolteotl.

15)   Eagle – CUAUGTLI

Bears the number 15 and the colour silver.
Those born under the sign of the Eagle are
strong, courageous and virile. Those born
under the sign of the Eagle have been
blessed with a lucid mind and a constantly
renewing energy. Their courage, strength
and bravery are very seductive.... so what

out lol! The Sun represents this sign and
its divine force is Xipe Totec.

16)   Vulture –
COZCAQUAUTLI

Bears the number 16. Those born under
the sign of the Vulture are blessed with
good health, and long life. They are very
responsible people, and will always
consider all avenues and their
consequences before taking action. Those
born under the sign of the Vulture make
shrewd business men and women, who will
calmly work toward any goal. The Sun is
associated with this sign and its divine
force is Itzpapalotl.

17)   Earthquake – OLLIN

Bears the number 17. Those born under
the sign of Earthquake are wise and
cautious with a strong sense of justice.
They are beautiful people both inside and
out. Those born under the sign of
Earthquake have a fantastically vivid
imagination which is paired with a daring
and energetic flair that is unique to them.
The Sun is associated with this sign and its
divine force is Xoltotl.

18)   Silex – TECPATL

Bears the number 18 and the colour Red.
Those born under the sign of the Silex are
extremely law-abiding and moral, and
believe in justice. They have a strong
abhorrence to lies and liars. Those born
under the sign of the Silex tend to go

through life with little to no complaint, and at times can become authoritarian from time to time. The planet Mercury is associated with this sign and its divine forces are Tezcatlipoca and Chalchiuhtotolin.

19)   Rain – QUIHUTL

Bears the number 19 and the colour dark red. Those born under the sign of Rain are passionate and tend to act on a whim, letting their passions carry them away, having their impulses guiding them. Those born under the sign of the Rain are versatile, adapting to situations if or when they change. The planet Mercury is associated with this sign and its divine forces are Tonatluh and Chantico.

20)   Flower – XOCHITL

Bears the number 20 and the colour white. Those born under the Flower are artistic, crazy, tender and very sensitive. Those born under the sign of the Flower are full of life and vigour. They may seem like odd balls to others signs, but they always have a kind word for others and a smile. The planet Venus is associated with this sign and its divine force is Xochiquetzal.

Egyptian Astrology Zodiac

In Ancient Egypt the gods had influence over the behaviour and fate of all mankind,

pharaoh, priest or commoner. These
influences can be seen in each of the signs
of their Zodiac.

The Nile	1st to 7th January 19th to 28th June 1st to 7th September
Osiris	1st to 10th March 27th November to 18th December
Thoth	1st to 19th April 8th to 17th November
Horus	20th April to 8th May 12th to 19th August
Amon-Ra	8th to 21st January 1st to 11th February
Geb	12th to 28th February 20th to 31st August
Anubis	9th to 27th May 29th June to 13th July
Sekhmet	29th July 11th August 30th October to 7th November
Isis	11th to 31st March 18th to 29th October 19th to 31st December
Bastet	14th to 28th July 23rd to 27th September 3rd to 17th October
Seth	28th May to 18th June 28th September to 2nd October
Mut	22nd to 31st January 8th to 22nd September

__Characteristics of the Signs__

The Nile

Those born under the sign of the Nile are very tolerant and pragmatic people. Those born under the sign of the Nile like to establish peace among others and will try to avoid any kind of conflict. They are dreamers and like to dream about all of the possibilities. They are passionate about nature and the world around them. They can be easily ruled by their emotions and passions, but sometimes these passions can get the best of them.

Osiris

Those born under the sign of Osiris have two sides to their personality; on one side they are strong, passionate and feisty but on the other they are vulnerable and indecisive. Those born under the sign of Osiris find it hard to what the right course of action when they are faced with challenges. They are optimistic about the future and can be misunderstood easily due to their dual natural.

Thoth

Those born under the sign of Thoth are fantastic puzzle and problem solvers. They are very creative and expressive and love sharing everything they have learned with others. Those born under the sign of the Thoth are often inspired to become teachers or a career where they are able to share wisdom and knowledge. They are extremely organised, and can be perfectionists. Those born under the sign of Thoth are humble and trusting.

Horus

Those born under the sign of Horus are
very courageous; they are risk takers;
especially when they are working to
achieve a goal. They are charismatic and
motivated, striving to achieve their goals.
Those born under the sign of Horus rarely
– if ever – let an opportunity pass them by
for fear of failure. They take great pride
themselves on being risk takers and
blazing trials.

Amon-Ra

Those born under the sign of Amon-Ra are
optimists and incredibly talented. They
make very good leaders; they have a knack
of inspiring others while making them feel
comfortable. Those born under the sign of
Amon-Ra are extremely giving and will
always give their best to anyone in need. In
any situation they will always be in control,
and confident which helps to comfort
others.

Geb

Those born under the sign of Geb are very
sensitive; they have kind hearts and in
touch with the feelings and needs of people
around them. Those born under the sign of
Geb tend to be introverted and intuitive
which allows them to have a great capacity
for compassion. They can be seen as over
emotional from time to time, but their
sensitive nature is what draws people to
them, regardless of their faults.

Anubis

Those born under the sign of Anubis have creativity and passion pouring from them. They prefer solitude and their own company, especially when they are working; they would rather be in a quiet place than a Those born under the sign of Anubis are very intense and their emotions match this which means they can be a little emotionally unpredictable.

Sekhmet

Those born under the sign of Sekhmet have two sides to their personalities. On one hand they're extremely disciplined and strict, but in contrast on the other hand they are very free and will go with the flow happily. Those born under the sign of Sekhmet can be unpredictable, as you never know which side of their personality; sometimes it can be like talking to two different people.

Isis

Those born under the sign of Isis are straight forward, and prefer to get to the point; they won't beat about the bush in a straightforward manner, which allows them to avoid misunderstandings. Those born under the sign of Isis are motivated by love, and having love in their lives. They are confident in their love lives and like adventure with their partners.

Bastet

Those born under the sign of Bastet are eternal seekers of peace and balance; they will strive to be surrounded by peace. They will instinctively avoid confrontation and will steer clear of stressful situations. Those born under the sign of Bastet are innately introverted preferring to be in quiet places rather than in large crowds and noisy places.

Seth

Those born under the sign of Seth seek change and adventure; they like to be challenged by new situations. They have a desire to feel complete, and their adventures are a way for them to find it. Those born under the sign of Seth are perfectionists and won't let anything hinder their journey to find completeness. They will pursue them until they found it.

Mut

Those born under the sign of Mut are naturally very protective and nurturing. They will protect anyone in their care, but will always go the extra mile for those they love. Those born under the sign of Mut have very strong parental instincts and make fantastic role models for the young.

Section 4

Days of the Week

Each day of the week has its own unique energy
that corresponds with planets, colours, elements,
crystals, incense, and etcetera. Pagans, Witches,
Wiccans choose to use these correspondences to
guide their day, their activities and their spiritual
working. The information contained here has been
gathered from many sources and compiled in an
easy to follow manner; the information for
correspondences is pretty standard across the
board, but from time to time one source will have
another interpretation or different information
from other sources. When it comes to following
correspondences I would advise reading them
thoroughly, but when it comes to putting this into
practice it is important to use what works for you,
your energy and the spell, ritual or magical
working you wish to do; don't be afraid to
improvise and wing it. If it work for you, that's all
that matters.

Aside from general correspondences, I have
gathered information about where the origin of the
name comes from, as well examples of the work
you can do with each day's energy.

Sunday

Sunday comes from the Old English Sunnandaeg
which literally means "day of the Sun".
Sunday Correspondences
Celestial Body: The Sun
Element: Fire
Gender: Masculine
Deities: Apollo, Brighid, Helios, Ra
Colours: Amber, Orange, Red, Gold, Yellow
Crystals: Amber, Diamond, Citrine, Holden
Healer, Carnelian, Sunstone, Tiger's Eye, Yellow
Topaz
Herbs/Plants: Angelica, Buttercup, Cinnamon,
Juniper, Eyebright, St John's Wart, Sunflower
Incense: Cedar, Cinnamon, Frankincense, Lemon,
and Sun Oil.
Energies & Associations: Agriculture, Beauty,
Creativity, Ego , Fame, Fatherly Love, Masculine

Energy Work, God Spells and Rituals, Health, Hope, Masculine Health, Power, Success, Achievement, Self-Expression, Spiritual Connection, Victory and Wealth.

Other Information:

- Many consider Sunday being the start of the week, and they believe that Sunday will set the tone for the rest of the week. With this in mind, ensure that Sunday's are full of light and happiness.
- Sunday is associated with our closest Star, the Sun.
- Sunday's are for personal growth and achievement, so working towards your own goals on a Sunday will help give you a boost.
- Gold has a strong association with the Sun, so wear gold coloured clothing, accessories or gold jewellery to tap into Sunday's solar energies.
- Sunflowers and Marigolds around your home to promote prosperity.
- Baking or cooking with Cinnamon while adding the intention for health and success.
- Oranges are associated with the Sun, and full of Vitamin C, so snacking on them will give you a nice boost.

Monday

Monday comes from the Old English Monandaeg, and known as "Day of the Moon" and in Latin is Dies Lunae.

Celestial Body: The Moon

Element: Water

Gender: Feminine

Deities: Artemis, Diana, Luna, Selene, Thoth.

Colours: White, Silver, Grey and Blue.

Crystals: Aquamarine, Moonstone, Mother of Pearl, Opal, Pearl, Quartz, Sapphire, Selenite and Silver.

Herbs: Chamomile, Catnip, Comfrey, Lily, Lotus, Mint, Moonflower, Moonwort, Myrrh, Poppy, Sage, Sandalwood and Willow.
Incense: Honeysuckle, Jasmine, Moon Oil, Sandalwood and Wormwood.
Energies & Associations: Clairvoyance, Divination, Dream Recall and Interpretation, Emotional Healing, Faerie Magic, Feminine Health and Hygiene, Female Fertility, Goddess Rituals, Invocations' and Spells, Hearth and Home Magic, Family Magic, Illusions, Intuition, Insight, Psychic Abilities, Purity, Wisdom, Women's Mysteries.
Other Information:

- Monday is closely associated with the Moon and all types of Lunar Magic.
- The Moon's association with the Feminine energies means that Monday's are good days to do magical work relating to womanhood.
- The Egyptian God Thoth is the God of Wisdom, so when you are looking for insight or wisdom. The Greek Goddess Selene is good to turn to when requiring aid in magical work.
- Silver, White and Pearlescent colours are closely associated with the Moon, so wearing silver coloured clothes, accessories or jewellery.
- Plant a garden on a Monday that is associated with the Moon such as Jasmine, Roses and Moonflower.
- Eat Melons under the calm and serene energies of the Moon.
- Brew a cup of Chamomile tea at night and charge with the Moon's energy to help bring a peaceful night's sleep.

Tuesday

Tuesday comes from the Old English Tiwesdaeg, or Tyr's Day, and in Latin is Dies Martis which means Day of Mars.
Celestial Body: Mars

Element: Fire
Gender: Masculine
Deities: Ares, Lilith, Mars, Morrigan, Tiwaz, Tyr.
Colour: Red, Black, Orange
Crystals: Bloodstone, Flint, Garnet, Iron, Pink Tourmaline, Rhodonite, Ruby and Steel.
Herbs: Allspice, Basil, Cactus, Chilli Pepper, Cornflower, Dragon's Blood, Garlic, Ginger, Holly, Horseradish, Mustard, Stinging Nettle, Onion, Pepper, Pine, Radish, Thistle, Tobacco.
Incense: Basil, Black Pepper, Dragon's Blood, Ginger, Pine and Patchouli
Energies & Associations: Aggressions, Breaking Negative Patterns and Spells, Competition, Courage, Defence, Ego, Dominance, Force, Hunting, Initiation, Leadership, Lust, Masculine Energy, Marriage, Power, Protection, Powerful Wards, Romance, Victory, war, conflict, Sex, Strength and Victory.
Other Information:

- Tuesday is associated with Mars, and as the Roman God of War Tuesday's are an opportune time to tap into energies of Strength and Courage, especially if you are faced with challenging situations.

- Wear fiery colours with your clothing, accessories or jewellery to compliment the energy of Tuesday's to turn a few heads.

- To reinforce your conviction during tasks, wear or carry a Bloodstone.

- To strengthen your protective wards work with fiery plants such as Snapdragon, and Thistle; both protective energies on their own.

- Make a meal with Carrots, Peppers and Garlic to empower yourself with prosperity, victory and success.

Wednesday

Wednesday comes from the Old English Wodensdaeg, and Woden or Odin's Day – Odin was the leader of the Gods for the Anglo-Saxon and Norse Pantheon.

Wednesday Correspondences

Celestial Body: Mercury

Element: Air

Gender: Masculine

Deities: Athena, Hermes, Lugh, Mercury, Odin/Woden.

Colours: Yellow, Silver, Grey, Purple, Orange.

Crystals: Agates, Amber, Aventurine, Citrine, Lapis Lazuli, Mercury, Pumice, Sodalite, Zinc.

Herbs: Aspen Tree, Fern Trees, Lavender, Lilies, Periwinkle.

Incense: Eucalyptus, Jasmine, Lavender, Sweet Pea

Energies & Associations: Gaining Answers, the Arts, Business Transactions, Chance, Charisma, Communication, Creativity, Debt Payment and Consolidation, Divination, Education and Learning, Facing Fears, Flexibility, Fortune, Gambling, Luck, Mental Health, Psychic

Work, Study, Summoning, Spirits,
Teaching, Travel, Work and Writing.

Other Information:

- Wednesday is associated with Mercury and with Communication, Change and Creativity. Mercury is the Roman Messenger God, his Greek counterpart is Hermes.
- Wear Orange, Purple accessories, clothing or jewellery to being a little of Wednesday's magic into your day.
- Agate is a fantastic multi-purpose crystal, and Wednesday's are great for working with Agate.
- For spells and charms for change and transformation. Use Ferns to reinforce and bolster protection spells, charms and wards. Aspen is fantastic for communication, especially when things are getting muddled up.
- Call upon Mercury or Hermes on a Wednesday night to facilitate movement and good luck.

Thursday

Thursday comes from the Old English Punresdaeg, and the day of Thor the Norse God of Thunder.

Thursday Correspondences

Celestial Body: Jupiter

Element: Earth

Gender: *Masculine*

Deities: Juno, Jupiter, Thor, Zeus

Colours: Blue, Green, Purple, Rich and Royal Colours.

Crystals: Aventurine, Amethyst, Jasper, Green Tourmaline, Lapis Lazuli, Malachite, Peridot, Tin and Turquoise

Herbs: Anise, Borage, Cinquefoil, Clove, Dill, Dandelion, Fig, Honeysuckle, Hyssop, Maple, Meadowsweet, Mint, Nutmeg, Oak, Patchouli, Sage and Star Anise

Incense: Cinnamon, Clove, Jupiter Oil, Musk, Nutmeg, Oakmoss, Sage, Patchouli.

Energy & Associations: Abundance, Career, Employment, Energetic Increase, Expansion, Generosity, Growth, Happiness, healing, Harvesting, Leadership, Honesty, Honour, Legal Matters, Loyalty, Masculine Fertility, Opportunities, Material Matters, Money, Optimism, Power, Prosperity, Wealth and Protection.

Other Information:

- Thursday is associated with the Roman God Jupiter, and he is associated with Prosperity, Abundance and Good Health.
- Thursday is named after the Norse God of Thunder, Thor, and he gave many of his attributes to Thursday's such as Strength and Abundance.

- Wear Rich colours such as Navy or Royal Blues, Deep Greens and luxurious Purples.
- Wearing or carrying Turquoise jewellery to attract healing and protective energies.
- Call on Thor when doing any spells or creating charms and amulets for abundance. Call on Jupiter to referee a fight or a situation fairly.
- Oak leaves in your spells or charms will give them a fair boost, and Oak is sacred to Gods associated with Thursday.

Friday

Friday comes from the Old English Frigdaeg, and Freya's or Frige's Day. Frige is the Norse Goddess of beauty, and eventually would become Frigg in later stories from the Poetic Edda; she is also connected to Freya.

Friday Correspondences

Celestial Body: Venus

Element: Water

Gender: Feminine

Deities: Aphordite, Eros, Freya, Frigg, Venus

Colours: Aqua, Coppery Colours, Green, Light Blue, Pink

Crystals: Aventurine, Blue Lace Agate, Copper, Coral, Emerald, Jade, Lapis Lazuli, Malachite, Moonstone, Quartz, Rose Quartz, Selenite

Herbs: African Violet, Apples and Apple Blossom, Barley, Apricot, Birch, Cardamom, Carnation, Catnip, Feverfew, Foxglove, Geranium, Heather, Hibiscus, Iris, Lilac, Rose, magnolia, Strawberry, Sweet pea, Thyme

Incense: Cardamom, Rose, Saffron, Sandalwood, Vanilla, Yarrow and Venus Oil.

Energy & Associations: the Arts, Beauty, Birth, Fertility, Friendship, Growth, Harmony, Birth, Fertility, Love, Marriage, Relationships, Music, Nature, Peace, Passion, Perfume, Love, Platonic Love, Pleasure, Reconciliation, Relationship Issues, Romance, Sexuality, Social Activities and Situations, Transformations.

Other Information:

- Friday is associated with the Roman Goddess of Love and her Greek counterpart Aphrodite; it is actually sacred to many Gods and Goddesses of Love. This means Friday's are the best days to work on your relationships.
- Wear Pink and Turquoise shades to bring a little of Friday's colour magic. You can do this by wearing clothing, accessories and jewellery.

- Rose Quartz and Turquoise are great stones to wear or carry to work with the energies of Friday. Wearing or carrying Rose Quartz will send out gentle loving energy to your surroundings.
- Use flower power in your magic by enchanting a pink rose for friendship and love; keep it in your home or take it with you to work (if you can)
- Call on Eros to being some passion into your life, or you can burn Rose scented or pink candles to being you a loving energies.

Saturday

Saturday is named after the Roman God Saturn and in mythology he was the First God of the Capitol, and has been known for Ancient Times as Saturnus Mons.

Saturday Correspondences

Celestial Body: Saturn

Element: Fire and Earth

Gender: Feminine

Deities: Cronos, the Fates, Hecate, Loki, Saturn

Colours: Purple, Black, Maroon, Indigo and many other Dark Colours.

Crystals: Apache Tear, Onyx, Coal, Coral, Hematite, Jet, Lead, Obsidian, Pewter, Smoky Quartz, and Tourmaline.

Herbs: Amaranth, Beetroot, Belladonna, Comfrey, Cypress, Hellebore, Hemlock, Hemp, Ivy, Moss, Mullein, Quince, Skullcap, Thyme.

Incense: Cypress, Myrrh, Patchouli, and Saturn Oil

Energy & Associations: Agriculture, Apprehension, Binding, Banishment, Boundaries, Caution, Cleansing, Creativity, Cursing, Care of the Elderly, Destruction magic, Endings, exorcism, Freedom, Fortune, Hexing, Hope, Limitations, Longevity, Meditation, Overcoming Obstacles, Protection, Psychic Defence, Revealing the Truth, Spiritual Communication.

Other Information:

- Saturday is associated with the Roman God Saturn, and some consider that Saturday is the last day of the week.
- Traditionally Saturdays are the best day for protection spells, charms, wards and amulets, but also fantastic for banishing negative energies. Saturday's are also fantastic for cleaning up any "messy" situations, especially if you have been ignoring them
- Dark colours such as dark purple, deep blue and black are closely associated to the energy of Saturday; and wearing clothing these colours, wearing accessories or jewellery.
- Lighting a Black candle and letting it burn will absorb negativity, and burning a purple candle to boost spirituality and spiritual wisdom.

- Cleanse and clean your home, tap into the obstacles that are around and remove their energy, making room for positive energies.
- You can call on Hecate for protection and Guidance.

Section 5

Birthstones

Background of Birthstones

We've all heard of birthstones and come across them at some point, and with this article I am going to look at birthstones in general but also look where the concept came from and what kind of magic van be woven using birthstones.

What are birthstones?

Birthstones are precious or semi-precious stones and crystals that are associated with the month that you are born or your zodiac signs. Each crystal has its own powerful metaphysical properties, and while in the corresponding month these properties are amplified giving them a little more oomph.

Where and when did birthstones originate?

The concept of birthstones has been around for a very long time and initially was given as gifts to bring good luck on the day you were born. In Tibet, a type and a type of healing from India called Ayurvedic birthstones have been used, studied and taught for thousands of years. The

Traditional birthstones as we know it has been used since the 15th Century, however the modern birthstone list was first created in 1912 by the American National Association of Jewellers in an attempt to bring a standardized list for jewellers. The difference between the traditional and modern lists of birthstones is their core reason for being created. The traditional list is purely based on the societal constructs and traditions of the time period in which they are created. The modern list was created by jewellers to bring a set order to birthstones, making a list that all jewellers could work from.

<u>**Traditional Birthstone List**</u>
January - Garnet
February - Amethyst
March - Bloodstone
April - Diamond
May - Emerald
June - Pearl
July - Ruby
August - Sardonyx
September - Sapphire
October – Tourmaline
November - Citrine
December - Turquoise

<u>Properties and Meanings of Birthstones</u>

January

The Birthstone for January is Garnet

Over the long centuries Garnets have been a stone associated with commitment and love. Garnets hold a powerful Red energy which not only inspires love and loyalty but as it connects to the Base Chakra it also inspires Passion. Garnets can be used to enhance intimacy, sensuality and sexuality in relationships. As with other red crystals Garnets boost your energy levels and assist you when working on your self-confidence and self-worth. Its connection to the Base Chakra means Garnets are protective and grounding stones too; that help to activate and strengthen your survival instincts by sharpening perceptions and alleviating fears or worries. Especially with those that are keeping you from moving forward.

Garnets are a fantastic purifier for the whole body, helping the body to absorb vital nutrients. It also helps to stimulate the body's natural metabolism. Garnets are also known to stimulate a healthy anti-body creation allowing the body to fend off or fight inflection. Over the many centuries Garnets have been used to increate and stimulate fertility. On an emotional level Garnets help you to let go of what is no longer working for you to identify any unhealthy or destructive behaviours and aid in their release.

When it comes to baneful energy Garnets will protect you, but they will also bounce that negative energy back to its origins. Garnets are particularly useful if you have been burned by negative gossip or lies as this will be bounced back and your own personal shields will benefit from the raw Red energy of the Garnet. When you meditate with Garnet focus on what you are passionate about whether it be a cause, job, hobby or venture. Garnets are also known to enhance physical endurance so if you need to physically exert yourself Garnets are great to work with

February

The Birthstone of February is Amethyst.

Amethyst has been long prized as a precious gemstone, it's been utilised as a gorgeous adornment in jewellery or as an amulet to famously help prevent drunkenness. Its name actually means 'non-intoxicating'. The use of Amethyst has been recorded as far back as Ancient Egypt where it is mentioned in the Book of the Dead; in which it mentions placing an Amethyst heart on the body of the deceased to ensure their passage to the afterlife is peaceful. In Christianity Amethyst is associated with purity and are often worn by members of the Roman Catholic clergy, Bishops in particular. In China Amethyst would be given to those who are involved in legal proceedings. During the Middle Ages Amethyst would be worn by soldiers and guards not only to protect them from harm or death, but to repel evil spirits.

Amethyst is a powerful Purple ray crystal that is known as a stone of spirituality. Amethyst has a wonderfully soothing energy for the wearer and those who are in their vicinity too. The energy of Amethyst can calm fears, lift the spirits and raises hopes as well as soothing anger and hot-headedness. Amethyst is a stone of change, transmuting negative energies into more beneficial energy; it also is a powerful stone of personal and spiritual transformations. Amethyst is a great amulet for those who travel to protect against psychic attacks, sickness, harm, drunkenness and the effects of baneful magic.

Amethyst helps to develop your psychic abilities by stimulating the right side of the brain allowing you to see through illusions to the truth. When you meditate with Amethyst you can develop your intuition, channelling your energy to a higher level which helps you to develop a deeper connection to Cosmic and Spiritual Energies. A geode, a natural cluster or a grouping of raw amethyst points will cleanse and restore other crystals that are placed upon them. Amethyst itself can be cleansed and recharged during a Full Moon.

March

The Birthstone of March is Aquamarine

Aquamarine is a stone that has always had close ties to the water element as its cooling blue-green colour evokes visions of crystal clear beaches of tropical islands. The name Aquamarine means 'Water of the Sea' which itself makes it a stone for sailors or people on sea voyages to promote safety while out at sea. Aquamarine helps to tap into your inner well of knowledge by letting the waters flow through you from the depth of yourself.

Aquamarine is a stone of compassion and emits a very compassionate energy which can bring a deep sense of calm and relaxation. Aquamarine will help to increase and heighten your awareness of the truth on all levels; especially when bringing to light things that have been hidden. Aquamarine also helps you to uncover unknown causes that affect situations, this will allow you to learn from it and eventually master the lessons. If you like make sure you are prepared for every eventuality, Aquamarine is a stone for you, and the stone will also help those who are easily overwhelmed. Aquamarine has flexibility to its energy which will help with acceptance rather than being judgmental. It will also help to renew your spirit giving you a fresh zest for life.

Aquamarine features in ancient stories of sea witches who cleansed the gemstone in the waters of the oceans while the Full Moon hung in the sky; and it's from stories such as these that tie Aquamarine to deities of the sea such as Poseidon. Aquamarine is said to counteract darkness and negativity, it also helps to quieten the conscious mind so you can develop your psychic abilities and the ability to trust your instincts. Aquamarine is said to be best cleansed with sea water and the Full Moon

April

The Birthstone of April is Diamond

Diamond is the hardest mineral on Earth and considered to be the most precious gemstone in the world. Diamonds have gained prestige because of the lustre, clarity and the spectacular fiery colour-play. The word Diamond means 'invincible' or 'indestructible' which has the hardest mineral on Earth is quite fitting. One of the outer planets has rain that is comprised of Diamonds. Diamonds have been given at marriage because they instill trust and fidelity; they also represent innocence and purity.

In the ancient world diamonds weren't worn as sparkling cut gems, they were worn as raw as raw unaltered stones and were treasured for their beauty in their natural form. It wasn't until many centuries later in the 17th Century that their hidden beauty was revealed, but their beauty was still secreted away, and it wasn't until 1919 when Marvel Tolkowsky created the round brilliant cut for diamonds. Diamonds are really useful gemstones when you want to clear away obstacles within the personal energy field. They are also fantastic for increasing self-respect and self-love. The diamond is an amazing tool when you are trying to understand your own emotional blockages.

Diamonds are known as a 'Master Healer' crystal, and like Quartz diamonds can be used to relieve almost every ailment. Diamonds are connected to the Crown Chakra, which activates and stimulates that energy centre. Diamonds are considered to be a gemstone of phenomenal power that will enhance the energy of other crystals working on the mind, body and spirit. Diamonds are often associated with the Sun because of its age, strength and hardness. Diamonds cab be used in spells, rituals and healing sessions to increase the strength of the activity; they are also closely associated with protection for the same reason.

Diamonds shouldn't be charged or cleansed, but I am looking more into that.

May

The Birthstone for May is Emerald.

The luxurious green of the Emerald is thanks to the presence of Chromium and Vanadium as the gemstone was formed, and like some other gemstones Emeralds are full of imperfections and to improve the clarity Emeralds are enhanced by oil in the search for flawlessness. Emeralds have long been known to be gemstones of protection while travelling as well as stones of messengers. This has lead Emerald to be associated with Mercury and Hermes, just two messenger gods.

Emerald is a tome of romance and deep love, helping to bring joy and happiness into your life; while it helps to enhance the memory and clairvoyant gifts. Emeralds are sacred to the Roman Goddess of Love – Venus. It's a crystal that works really well with the energy of the Heart Chakra. Emeralds work on preserving love and have been a symbol of hope for many centuries. For many; Emeralds act as a balm for a troubled mind, bringing logic and reason to the wearer. Emerald is a really good stone for communicating with withers with love and honesty – speaking from the heart can be daunting sometimes, and Emeralds can help relieve this.

Emeralds can help the recovery process after infections and infectious illnesses; it also has a detoxifying nature which helps the body rid itself of unwanted toxins. The energy of the Emerald can helps to strengthen the heart and the immune system. Emeralds help to bring love into your life by opening you up to new opportunities and energies you may not normally open yourself up to. Traditionally Emeralds have been used to protect against all kinds of enchantments as well as those who choose to use baneful magic.

Emeralds can be helpful when wanting to increase intuitive abilities and creativity, allowing the creativity flow freely.

June

The Birthstone for June is Pearl

Pearl's aren't your run-of-the-mill gemstone because they are actually an organic compound from a defence system against irritants inside shellfish such as oysters and mussels. This defence system activates when an irritant such as a speck of dirt or sand gets inside the shell. The Oyster (or Mussel) will secrete a layer of a substance called Nacre to surround the irritant. The layers will build up and form a Pearl. When light hits the overlapping layers is when the Pearl's magical lustre really comes to life. Pearls symbolize purity, innocence and faith; they are known to enhance personal integrity too. Pearls help to clear your mind before meditation so you mind is clean and clear for picking up messages from Spirit or the Universe. It's said that Cleopatra only drank wine with crushed pearls in to protect from being poisoned.

Pearls are closely connected to both the Moon and the oceans. They are also very strongly associated with sincerity, honesty, truth and integrity. Wearing pearls can help you attune yourself with the "flow of life" but will also act as an anchoring point which will allow you to reflect on your energy and your actions. For centuries Pearls have been a symbol for purity; fostering a charitable nature along with a high degree of personal integrity – meaning if you say something you will follow it through. Pearls work well to balance the energy and emotions of even the most watery of the star signs, Pearls are often considered to be the ultimate physical realisation of Divine Feminine Energy of the Universe. Pearls absorb energy like a sponge absorbs water so pearls should always be worn with caution; how you feel while you are working with pearls is the energy they will absorb and store until they are cleansed and used again.

The use of pearls for magical purposes can be divided into two separate schools of thought. The first is that because they originated from a living creature they carry a debt of life for their removal and potential harm to the creature. The second is that because they originate from a living creature they carry the energy of the living being, making it one of the more powerful substances to work with.

July

The Birthstone for July is Ruby

Rubies have always been gemstone connected to various myths, legends and tales about heroes and great deeds. It's been closely associated with royalty for centuries. The Black Prince Ruby features in the Imperial State Crown and has been owned by the Royal Family since 1367, and Henry VIII was the one who placed it in the crown (the BPR isn't technically a Ruby as was believed since 1367, it's actually a Spinel) The Black Prince Ruby is an uncut natural stone rather than a faceted, highly polished gem. It's said that when Henry VIII decided to divorce Catherine of Aragon the Ruby she wore religiously became dark and lost its spectacular shine. According to Hinduism Rubies are said to hold an unquenchable fire that no man could ever extinguish.

Rubies bring a little fire into your life while giving you the courage to follow your dreams or to discover what brings you bliss. Rubies are an injection of energy in your life, especially when you feel like your energy is hitting the floor. Rubies help to expand your awareness beyond the self allowing you to see of what is going on around you. Rubies are a sign of status, wealth and abundance; wearing, carrying or keeping Rubies will help to maintain these things. If you are prone to (self) destructive behaviour, Ruby will help you to acknowledge this and give you the strength to overcome the conditioning that made you that way; helping you to resist the urges.

Rubies are marvellous at shielding you against negative energies and energy vampires; they work best on the heart chakra's energy as Rubies are connected to the matters of the heart, Rubies help to remove self-imposed limitations as well as those that others have placed upon you. Rubies help to foster your natural leadership skills by giving your courage a little boost while fostering selflessness. When you feel like your energy is dropping Rubies and help you regain control and a little of what has been lost.

August

The Birthstone for August is Peridot

Peridot is a quizzical gem as it's found in one colour but has more than one name. There are three main varieties of Peridot; an olive-green variety that is known as Ovaline. A yellow-green variety of Peridot is known as Chrysolite. Lastly; a bright green variety is known as Peridot. The green characteristics of the stone is due to trace amounts of iron; the amount of iron deposits change the intensity of green and it's shade and appear from an earthy brown-greens to a spring-like green to a fresh, airy and joyous yellow-green.

Peridot has a happy uplifting and joyous energy bringing happiness into your life. Peridot is a heart chakra stone and as such Peridot can help cleanse the heart of negative emotions, but also helps you to leave your ego behind. This can help immensely with friendships and relationships. Peridot has a great ability as a healer for the whole body. It's a motivator and will help you pull your socks up and get on with what you need to do. Peridot assists you at looking at the past to see the lesson or reward from your previous experiences then helps you to move forward making positive

changes as you go. If you're unsure or afraid
Peridot can help relieve you these but supporting
you and fostering strength and courage. The
Romans would wear or carry Peridot to protect
them from enchantments or baneful magic or
illusions designed to mislead.

Peridot is a stone that has been called a Stone of
Fortune as it can be helpful in attracting
abundances in income, love, luck and general
happiness. Peridot, like Garnet can reflect bad
energy back to where it originated; leaving you
unaffected by it. Alongside it's repelling nature
Peridot is also great for warding off evil or negative
entities or spirits. Peridot is a gem that energy
healer's turn to when they need a helping hand,
and to replace the depleted energies.

September

The Birthstone for September is Sapphire

Sapphires are only second to diamonds in terms of
hardness which makes it the second hardest
mineral on Mother Earth. The legendary beauty
and strength has made Sapphires a very popular
gemstone among royalty from all corners of the
earth. It's said that kings wore Sapphires to
protect him from any jealous that could appear
within his court; as well as protecting him from
harm.
For centuries Sapphires have been a way to
protect against the evil eye, it was also used as a
way to protect against baneful magic and will send
it back to where it came; making Sapphires like
Garnets. Magicians, mystics, healers and
alchemists used Sapphires as a tool to focus,
direct and increase their spells or other works.
Sapphires are very useful when you want to open
up to messages from the higher realms; Sapphires
also help you clarify and understand messages
you have received. When you sit and meditate with
Sapphires you are able to discover and tap into
your own potential. If you are starting a new

venture or journey Sapphire can help you keep focused so you won't lose sight of your goal. Meditating with Sapphire once your venture begins will help you keep balance and perspective which will help you to stay organised and your mind uncluttered.

Sapphires are effective when you're healing the nervous system, but will also being clarity of mind for the person who is being healed; this helps them focus on the healing done, allowing healing on all levels

October

The Birthstone for October is Opal

Unlike many gemstones Opals have no crystalline structure because they are actually tiny spheres of hardened Silica Gel. Opals have a high water content, some pieces may have up to as much as 20% This high water content means that if an Opal isn't cared for carefully it can dry out and begin to crack. Opals form by cavities being filled in sedimentary or igneous rock. Opals have been known to replace "organic" matter in fossils, shells, wood and Opals have even been known to form in bones. There are two forms of Opal; the Precious Opal displays the amazing flashes of colour with an incredible iridescence. The Common Opal is typically opaque or milky in colour with little or no flash at all.

Opals are stones of increased inspiration, creativity and can help you to release your inhibitions allowing you to follow wherever your creativity takes you. Opals can be used to enhance your memory; meaning it's a good gemstone for students studying for exams. Opals are hardened Silica Gel which contain water and it is this very things that associates Opals closely with the water element. Opals can magnify feelings and emotions that may have been forgotten; with this amplification you may begin to be braver or more spontaneous, taking risks when it comes to the matters of the heart.

Opals come in a wide range of colours and each colour has its own name but all Opals have the same intrinsic properties; meaning when you use them individually they all carry the same underlying traits that make Opals so special. The wide range of colours also means that each Opal type will have its own characteristics as well as those that are common among all Opals. Opals can be programmed for almost any purpose or work with almost all kinds of energy. This makes Opals a valuable tool for spells, healing and other magical needs. Opals can be used for protection during Astral Projection or Shamanic Journeying.

November

The Birthstone for November is Topaz

Topaz has featured in history for at least as far back as Ancient Egypt where is said that its colour came from the golden light of the Sun God Ra. To the Egyptians this made Topaz a powerful amulet, protecting the wearer from harm....as long as they were faithful to Ra. The name Topaz comes from the Sanskrit word for "Fire" which ties in nicely to the Egyptians belief about Topaz being connected to Ra. There are legends saying that in the presence of poison or toxins a Topaz would change colour; however you need to use Topaz with care because it's abilities wax and wane with the cycle of the moon. While Topaz is a relatively hard gem but if it is hit hard enough it can be cleaved in two.

Topaz comes in a wide range of colours, and each has its own properties but they all Topaz crystals promote understanding, compassion and empathy. Topaz is a stone of success in all areas of your life from love to wealth, from creativity and intelligence. Topaz is fantastic for finding balance in your life, bringing calm to your thoughts and emotions; it also can be beneficial to stimulate the metabolism and digestive system.

Topaz has long been known to be used for protection, it can protect against envy or intrigue. It's also said that it can protect against disease, injury and even sudden death. Like many other gemstones Topaz will protect you from baneful magic. Having Topaz in your home can help ward against accidents; while having some under your pillow will fend of nightmares.

December

The Birthstone for December is Turquoise

Turquoise was one of the first minerals to be sustainably mined, and due to its intense colour it has been prized among many of the world's finest stones. The vivid and striking colours go from a sky blue to a deep blue-green colour. This variety of colour depends on the amount of Copper and Iron in the stone. The Ancient Egyptians prized Turquoise as a stone of life. Turquoise was used in jewellery and funerary regalia and one of the earliest examples is from a bracelet belonging to Queen Zar, who ruled in the early dynasties about 5,500 years ago.

Turquoise has a very complex process in which Copper is the vital component as it's what kick-starts the whole process. That aside Turquoise has been a stone with very close links to spirituality and spiritual matter for well over 7,000 years. Turquoise can be found all over the world but Peruvian is said to be the best of the best. Turquoise is a stone that will align and strengthen all of your chakras and while meditating with Turquoise you open yourself up to the Universal energy source, but it will also help you to attune yourself to the spiritual planes; providing protection during Astral Travel and Shamanic Journeying

More Information on Birthstones

Another list was created and adopted in Britain in 1937, and while there have been additions to the list in 1952, 2002 and 2016 there hasn't been a complete overhaul of an existing list or the creation of a new list since 1937.
In 1952 the American list was updated by adding Alexandrite for June, Pink Tourmaline for October and Citrine for November.
In 2002 the American was once again updated by adding Tanzanite for December.
In 2016 the list was updated once more by adding Spinel for August.

US Birthstone list as of 2016
January – Garnet
February – Amethyst
March – Aquamarine and Bloodstone
April – Diamond
May – Emerald
June – Pearl, Moonstone and Alexandrite
July – Ruby
August – Peridot and Spinel
September – Sapphire
October – Opal and Pink Tourmaline
November – Topaz and Citrine
December – Turquoise, Zircon and Tanzanite

UK Birthstone List as of 2013
January – Garnet
February – Amethyst
March – Aquamarine and Bloodstone
April – Diamond and Clear Quartz
May – Emerald and Chrysoprase
June – Pearl and Moonstone
July – Ruby and Carnelian
August – Peridot and Sardonyx

September – Sapphire and Lapis Lazuli
October – Opal
November – Topaz and Citrine
December – Tanzanite and Turquoise

Tibetan 'Mystical' Birthstone List

January – Emerald
February – Bloodstone
March – Jade
April – Opal
May – Sapphire
June – Moonstone
July – Ruby
August – Diamond
September – Agate
October – Jasper
November – Pearl
December – Zircon and Turquoise

Ayurvedic Birthstone List

January – Garnet
February – Amethyst
March – Bloodstone
April – Diamond
May – Agate
June – Pearl
July – Ruby
August – Sapphire
September – Moonstone
October – Opal
November – Topaz
December – Black Onyx

Astrological Birthstone List

Aries - Diamond, Bloodstone, Jasper and Topaz
Taurus - Sapphire, Amber, Coral, Emerald, Rose Quartz and Turquoise
Gemini - Agate, Chrysoprase, Citrine, Moonstone, Pearl and White Sapphire
Cancer - Emerald, Moonstone, Pearl and Ruby
Leo - Onyx, Carnelian, Sardonyx, Golden Topaz, and Tourmaline
Virgo - Carnelian, Jade, Jasper, Moss Agate, and Sapphire

Libra - Peridot, Lapis Lazuli, Opal and Chrysolite
Scorpio - Beryl, Apache Tear, Aquamarine, Coral
and Obsidian
Sagittarius - Topaz, Amethyst, Ruby, Sapphire and
Turquoise
Capricorn - Ruby, Agate, Garnet and Black Onyx
Aquarius - Garnet, Amethyst, Moss Agate, Opal
and Sugilite
Pisces - Amethyst, Aquamarine, Bloodstone, Jade,
Rock Crystal and Sapphire

"Birth Day" Stones

The term birthstone is sometimes used as a
synonym for birth day stones. Each day of the
week has its own associated crystals which are
separate from the stones associated with each
month.
Monday – Pearl and Rock Crystal
Tuesday – Ruby and Emerald
Wednesday – Amethyst and Lodestone
Thursday – Sapphire and Carnelian
Friday – Emerald and Tiger's Eye
Saturday – Turquoise and Diamond
Sunday – Diamond and Topaz

Each month of the year has characteristics that
each month has which correspond to why those
certain
crystals and stones have become associated with
that month.

Month and their Qualities

January – faith, eternity and truth
February – luck, wittiness and health
March – happiness and understanding
April – eternity, courage and health
May – fidelity, goodness and love
June – peace, nobility and beauty
July – love, enthusiasm and strength
August – success, peace and love
September – Serenity and Truth
October – purity, hope and health
November – Wisdom, Courage, Sincerity

December – love, happiness and luck

Birthstones can also be found in 3 of the popular world religions too.

Judaism

In Jewish tradition, there was once a connection between the months of the year, the signs of the zodiac and the twelve stones that appeared on the ceremonial breast plate of the high priest; and this breast plate was believed to represent the twelve tribes of Israel. Back in the 8th to 10th centuries these stones were also associated with the growing Christian movement and the twelve apostles and their names would be engraved into the stone with their virtues. In those times, all of the stones were kept and one stone was worn during the corresponding month. The tradition of only having one stone is actually a relatively new custom, and the stones that we use today have very few similarities to those of Jewish customs.

Hinduism

Birthstones can also be found in Hinduism, in a text called the Mani Mala, but I can't find much information on this outside of the months and their associated crystals.

January – Serpent Stone
February – Moonstone
March – Gold Shiva Lingam
April – Diamond
May – Emerald
June – Pearl
July – Sapphire
August – Ruby
September – Zircon
October – Coral
November – Tiger's Eye
December – Topaz

Christianity

As I previously mentioned birthstones have been associated with the twelve apostles, and the foundation stones of New Jerusalem. The gates were situated at each of the cardinal compass points, and within each 'quarter' contained 3 gates, making a total of twelve gates. The walls of New Jerusalem contained 12 foundation stones, and each of these foundation stones was engraved with the name of one of the apostles. These stones would be adorned with precious and semi-precious stones. Twelve is a powerful number in Christianity, the twelve apostles relating to the twelve foundation stones, the twelve gates and by extension the twelve tribes of Israel – Jesus was a Jew and not a Christian.

***Note** Each stone in the following lists have ties that can be traced back to the first temple era*

Original Version List

1st Foundation – Jasper
2nd Foundation – Sapphire
3rd Foundation – Chalcedony
4th Foundation – Emerald
5th Foundation – Sardonyx
6th Foundation – Carnelian
7th Foundation – Chrysoberyl
8th Foundation – Beryl
9th Foundation – Topaz
10th Foundation – Chrysoprase
11th Foundation – Jacinth (Zircon)
12th Foundation – Amethyst

New Version List

1st Foundation – Diamond
2nd Foundation – Lapis Lazuli
3rd Foundation – Turquoise
4th Foundation – Rock Crystal
5th Foundation – Agate
6th Foundation – Ruby
8th Foundation – Golden Quartz
9th Foundation – Topaz
10th Foundation - Malachite
11th Foundation – Emerald
12th Foundation – Amethyst

The twelve foundation stones not only carried the name of one of the apostles and encrusted in gems, but they were also given specific qualities which related to the qualities of Jesus Christ, and qualities he taught.

Stones and Qualities of Christ

Jasper – Satisfaction
Sapphire – The Soul
Chalcedony – The Truth
Emerald – Kindness and Goodness
Sardonyx – Strength
Carnelian – Readiness to Help
Chrysoberyl – Excellence of his Divine Nature
Beryl – Control of the Passions
Topaz – Uprightness
Chrysoprase – Sternness towards Sinners
Jacinth – Dignity
Amethyst – Perfection.

Section 6

Names of the Moon

Through the many cultures of the world the Moon has held sway, and each culture has given their own names to the Moon as it passes through the year and the seasons. There are many lists out there, the Celtic and the Native American lists are among the most well known of these lists. In this section you will see lists from a range of Native American Cultures, the Celts, a Colonial American, the Old English lists and a modern day Neo-Pagan variation. Through my research these are possibly the most frequently searched for and used.

Colonial American Names

- January – The Winter's Moon
- February – The Trapper's Moon
- March – The Fish Moon
- April – The Planter's Moon
- May – The Milk Moon
- June – The Rose Moon
- July – The Summer Moon
- August - Dog Day's Moon
- September – The Harvest Moon
- October – The Hunter's Moon
- November – The Beaver Moon
- December – The Christmas Moon

Cherokee Native American

- January – The Cold Moon
- February – The Bony Moon
- March – The Windy Moon
- April – The Flower Moon
- May – The Planting Moon
- June – The Green Corn Moon
- July – The Ripe Corn Moon
- August – The Fruit Moon
- September – The Nut Moon
- October – The Harvest Moon
- November – The Trading Moon
- December Moon – The Snow Moon

Choctaw Native American

- January – The Cooking Moon
- February – The Little Famine Moon
- March – The Big Famine Moon
- April – The Wild Cat Moon
- May – The Panther Moon
- June – The Windy Moon
- July – The Crane Moon
- August – The Women's Moon
- September – The Mulberry Moon
- October – The Blackberry Moon
- November – The Sassafras Moon
- December – The Peach Moon

Sioux Native American

- January – The Moon of the Terrible
- February – The Moon of the Racoon
- March – The Moon when Eyes are sore from Bright Snow
- April – The Moon when Geese Return in Scattered Formation
- May – The Moon when Leaves are Green
- June – The Moon when the Berries are Ripe
- July – The Moon of the Middle Summer
- August – The Moon when All Things Ripen

- September – The Moon when the Calves Grow Hair
- October – The moon when the Quilting and Beading is Done
- November – The Moon when Horns are Broken Off
- December – The Twelfth Moon

Celtic

- January – The Quiet Moon
- February – The Moon of Ice
- March – The Moon of Winds
- April – The Growing Moon
- May – The Bright Moon
- June – The Moon of Horses
- July – The Moon of Claiming
- August – The Dispute Moon
- September – The Singing Moon
- October – The Harvest Moon
- November – The Dark Moon
- December – The Cold Moon

English

- January – The Wolf Moon
- February – The Storm Moon
- March – The Chaste Moon
- April – The Seed Moon
- May – The Hare Moon
- June – The Dyan Moon

- July – The Rose Moon
- August – Lightening Moon
- September – The Barley Moon
- October – The Blood Moon
- November – The Snow Moon
- December – The Oak Moon

Neo-Pagan

- January – The Ice Moon
- February – The Snow Moon
- March – The Death Moon
- April – The Awakening Moon
- May – The Grass Moon
- June – The Planting Moon
- July – The Rose Moon
- August – The Lightening Moon
- September – The Harvest Moon
- October – The Blood Moon
- November – The Tree Moon
- December – The Long Night Moon

Section 7 – The Appendix

Colour Magic

Colour is a language, all of its own and like other forms of non-verbal languages, everything has a meaning.

If you look up the word 'colour' you'd find a
number of definitions, and even with all of them
combined they pale in comparison to the intricate
magic that is colour. The essence of colour cannot
truly be described with words because it's much
bigger than any language. There is no part of life
that light doesn't touch to some degree. It was
there at the dawn of creation, and will still be
present when the Universe breathes its last
breath.

Colour is more than just what we see with our
eyes. While we predominately process colour with
our eyes our bodies also process light via the
Hypothalamus and the Pineal Gland; so when we
see a colour that we love or hate you can have a
physical response or at least "feel" something
about that colour.

The light that we see comes from the Sun as
electromagnetic energy. The Electromagnetic
Spectrum displays the different kinds of
wavelengths. Most of the wavelengths are invisible
to our eyes; however wavelengths between 627
and 436 nanometres are able to be seen by the
naked eye, beyond this scientific equipment. Red
is the lowest and longest frequency of the visible
spectrum with Violet being the highest and
shortest frequency of the visible spectrum; all
electromagnetic energy is measured in
nanometres, centimetres, metres and kilometres.
At the lower end of the electromagnetic spectrum
the wavelengths are longer; below the visible
spectrum include radio waves which include FM
radio, TV, Radar Short-Wave Radio and Infrared
Rays. At the other side of the visible spectrum –
above Violet – there is Ultra-Violet Light, X-Rays,
Gamma Rays and Cosmic Rays.

The Visible spectrum is broken down into six or
seven wavelength measurements and we know

this better as the Rainbow. The nanometre measurement for each colour is:

- Red Light = 627-780 nanometres
- Orange Light = 589-627 nanometre
- Yellow Light = 556-589 nanometres
- Green Light = 495-556 nanometres
- Blue Light = 436-495 nanometres
- Violet Light = 380-436 nanometres
- ** Indigo Light** = This has been under dispute and most modern scientists don't have a separate listing for Indigo, they divide the spectrum between Blue and Violet. When Indigo was listed it was between 450 to 420 nanometres.

Colour Groups

Now that all the scientific stuff is out of the way, let's have a look at colour groups, and how they are connected.

Colour can be divided into three groupings; the first are the Primary Colours, second are the Secondary Colours and third are the Tertiary Colours. To understand these groups you need to think about them as pigments in the colour itself.

Primary Colour – The Primary Red, Blue and Yellow contain only one pigment. They haven't been mixed so it's pure colour, undiluted.

Secondary Colour – Secondary colours are essentially the offspring of pairings of the Primary Colours.

- Yellow + Red = Orange
- Red + Blue = Purple
- Blue + Yellow Green

Tertiary Colours – Tertiary colours are essentially the offspring of secondary colours. They are the result of a primary and the nearest secondary colour.

- Yellow + Orange = yellow/orange
- Red + Orange = red/orange
- Red + Purple = red/purple
- Blue + Purple = blue/purple
- Blue + Green = blue/green
- Yellow + Green = yellow/green

Understanding Colour

As mentioned before colour is a visible wavelength of light and as such they aren't static energies and the relationship we have with certain colours can change their meaning. The relationship can also effect whether the colour is negative or positive. For example; if someone was to wear pink to work one day, this could be for one or more of the meanings associated with the colour pink.

1 Pink is their favourite.

2 Maybe they want to surround themselves with unconditional love.

3 May feel the need to do something after gaining insight.

4 May feel over emotional and need the support that pink brings.

The response we have to colour stem from childhood associations or a preference for one colour the other. People don't always choose a colour they need, they often choose based on how much they like a certain colour; even if the colour is the opposite of the colour they really need. People tend to be attracted to a certain colour for a few reasons; their colour choice may be based on their favourite colour, based on their personality type, the conditions of which they are experiencing, unconscious desires or thought processes. **Some people will know exactly what colour they need, however there is equally as many people who don't have a clue, which is okay too.**

The Visible Spectrum

The Colour Red

Keywords:

The psychological meanings of Red are; Adventure, Aggression, Courage, Danger, Drama, Energy, Strength, Vitality, Heat, Warmth, Violence, War, Hatred, Passion and Determination. The Esoteric meanings of Red are Action, Ceremonial Magic, Ambition, Assertiveness, Desire, Sexuality, Sensuality, Passion, Leadership, Confrontation, Conflict, Determination to Succeed, Self-Confidence, Power, Potency and Willpower.

Red Correspondences

Higher Forces: The Mother stage of the Triple Goddess, Gods of War, God or Masculine Energy

Element: Fire

Zodiac: Aries, Capricorn, Gemini, Leo, Libra, Sagittarius, Scorpio and Taurus

Planets: Saturn and Mars

Chakras: Root Chakra

The Body: The Blood, Physical Energy, Strength, Prostate and the release of Adrenaline.

Red Crystals

Red Crystals includes; Fire Agate, Red Amethyst, Bloodstone, Dragon's Blood Calcite, Red Calcite, Cinnabar, Crocoite, Cuprite, Garnet, Almandine Garnet, Red Sandstone, Red Jasper, Mookaite, Harlequin, Quartz, Red Phantom Quartz, Rhodocrosite, Rhodonite, Ruby, Tiger Iron, Tugtupite, Vanadinite, Red Zircon and Zincite.

Red and Maroon Crystals can be used for;

(RED) Enhancing Action, Increasing Energy, Building Conviction, Developing Courage, Becoming Fearless, Growing Inner Strength, Success in Exploring the Unknown, Building Drive and Determination, Achieving Glory, Building a Sense of Self-Worth.

(DARK RED) Making a Relationship Serious, Bountiful Harvest, Building/Finding Devotion, and Building Passion in your life, Rewarding Effort, Finding a Soul mate and Dealing with Indifference.

About the Colour Red

The colour red is a raw energy, the colour of passion, action and sexuality. Red speaks of motivation, stimulation and will. Red is a primal energy, it's a strong and powerful masculine energy. Red is the colour of deep warmth and our most primal need to survive. Red is a strong-willed colour that will help bring confidence to the shy or those lacking in will-power.

Red is often associated with love, however red is actually closer to sexuality and lust than it is to love. Red is often used in restaurants because it stimulates the appetite and increases any cravings for food. Red is a colour that relates to physical strength, persistence, drive and personal power. Red is a super power of a colour and it has aggressive qualities which has connected it to war, combat and primal masculine energy. If you are surrounded by too much red you can become irritable, agitated or even angry due to its powerful energy. In China; red is a colour of good luck, and brides would traditionally wear red on their wedding day. Red is a very warm colour with a very extroverted character. It stimulates you energy and can combat feelings of sluggishness and procrastination. Red will get your adrenaline going. Red is closely connected to the physical body, especially with the heart, blood and circulation; red can help the production of Haemoglobin for new red blood cells. Red can be used to help those who have low blood pressure by raising it. The Ancient humans believed blood was the source of all the secrets to life. During the colder months of the year red can help to fend off the chills. By wearing red socks, gloves, vests or scarves can help warm up your body with its warming energy.

• Red is the colour of warmth, heat and burning. When we see red-hot or burning things it provokes caution or fear.

• Red can easily lead to excessive behaviours, because by its nature it is impulsive

• When a woman wears red she stands out, it's a "here I am, look at me"

• Red helps to promote physical desire

• Red speaks of passions about a belief, undertaking, issue or situation

• Red is closely related to passion and physical desire in all of its forms including sexual appetite and cravings.

• Red boosts your physical energy and increases your heart rate.

• Red is a get up and go colour, it can get your bottom moving.

Bring Red into your life when:

• There is a lack of energy

• There is a lack of enthusiasm

• There is a lack of interest in life

• There is an inability to make decisions

• There are feelings of insecurity and anxiety.

• Use Red when you want to be bold and dynamic, use red accessories such as ties, scarves, jewellery/cufflinks even nail polish

• Use Red when you need a boost to your confidence for things like a job interview or a social gathering. Accessories are a great way to bring the power of Red into your life.

The Colour Orange

Keywords:

The Psychological meanings of the colour Orange are; Activity, Child-Like, Appetite, Energy, Communication, Friendliness, Vitality, Sociable, Optimistic, Persuasion, Fun, Happiness, joy, Warmth, Heat, and Noisy. The Esoteric meanings of the colour Orange are; Abundance, Action, Happiness, Joy, Ambition, Career Goals, Lick, Encouragement, Creativity, Love, Sexuality, Harvest, Power, Prosperity, Enthusiasm, Motivation, Druid Magic, Authority, Appetite, Stimulating, Kindness, Legal matters and Justice, Mental Alertness, Power, Strength, Manifestation, Change and Persistence.

Orange Correspondences

Higher Power: Deities associated with Luck or Fortune and Deities and Spirits associated with Fire

Element: Fire

Days of the Week: Tuesday, Wednesday and Sunday

Times of the Year: Beltane, Lughnasadh, Mabon and Samhain

Season: Summer and Autumn

Zodiac: Cancer, Gemini, Leo, Libra and Sagittarius

Planet: The Sun and Mercury

Chakra: Sacral Chakra

The Body: Pelvis, Urinary System, Bladder, Digestion and Reproductive Organs

Magical Attributes: Confidence, Social Situations, Courage and Energy

Orange Crystals

Orange Crystals include; Orange Calcite, Orchid Calcite, Carnelian, Sunstone, Stilbite, Sardonyx, Vanadinite, Hessonite, Goldstone, Zincite, Amber, Aragonite, Tangerine Quartz, Tangerine Aura Quartz, Cancrinite, Celestobarite, Baked Amethyst, Spessartine Garnet, Hureaulite, Karibibite, Mookaite, Sphalerite, Stellerite, Orange Topaz, Imperial Topaz, Fire Opal, Fire Agate.

Orange Crystals can be used for;

(LIGHT ORANGE) Charm, Companionship, Encouragement, Friendship, Generosity, Kindness, Loyalty, Popularity, Praise, Selflessness, Overcoming Shyness, Dedication.

(ORANGE) Celebration, Enjoyment, Fulfilment, Joy, Merriment, Pleasure, Sex, Dealing With Depression, Overcoming Grief, Dealing with Sorrow.

(DARK ORANGE) Belonging, Benevolence, Community, Family, Good Reputation, Home, Hospitality, Marriage, Sense of Belonging, Support, Dealing with Abandonment, Cure for Homesickness, Dealing with Separation.

About the Colour Orange

Orange is a warm colour, but doesn't have the raw fiery energy that red has. Orange is closely associated with the life-giving energy of the sun. As Orange is an equal mixture of red and yellow, it combines the warmth and stimulation of Red with the cheery happiness of yellow. Orange is outgoing, enthusiastic, impulsive but constructive.

Orange relates to your instincts and the innate 'gut feeling' you may sometimes get; it is the 'we' sometimes associate with rejuvenation and optimism. Orange offers you emotional support and strength through difficult times such as disappointment, break-ups and even with the loss of someone. It can help with the supporting the journey to acceptance. Orange is a very positive colour, it helps to introduce positive and uplifting energies into your life Orange is an adventurers colour, so it's a colour that is often associated with risk-taking and thrill-seeking, and those who are always on the go. As Orange is a warm colour it's inviting, but also stimulating to your physical energy levels and to the mind. Orange is a great social colour as it helps to get you think and talking. For social gatherings like means or parties Orange is the perfect colour to relax your guests and get them talking, it will also get their juices flowing too. On the flipside if you are trying to lose weight or change your relationship with food, it's not a great colour to have in your kitchen, because like Red, Orange stimulates the taste buds.

• Orange has a more balanced energy that Red, not as aggressive but still full of vitality and rejuvenation.

• Orange is a strong and courageous colour; it helps to take action so you can move onward and upward through challenges.

• Socialising, friendship and community are closely associated with Orange.

• Orange warms without burning. The light of a sunrise or sunset encourage creative ideas and contemplative thought.

• The Fox cub illustrates perfectly how Orange embodies playful exploration and creativity.

• Orange is a balance of physical activity and mindful contemplation.

• Orange is enthusiastic, optimistic and extroverted.

Bring Orange into your life when:

• There is a feeling of bleakness.

• There is a feeling of boredom.

• There is a lack of interest in what you normally enjoy.

• There is an increase in taking yourself too seriously.

• There is a fear of feeling pleasure or enjoying sensuality.

• There is an inability to let go of the past.

• There is a problem moving forward from negative experiences.

• Use Orange during times of stress or after a significant shock as you can help bring your body back into a state of harmonious balance.

The Colour Yellow

Keywords:

The Psychological meanings of Yellow are Awareness, Betrayal, Caution, Easiness, Innovation, The Sun, Illumination, Warmth, Heat, Hospitality and Cowardice. The Esoteric Meanings of yellow are, Abundance, Creativity, Learning, Intellect, Action, Happiness, Joy, Hazards, Learning, Mental Clarity, Tests and Exams, Endurance, Awareness, Banishing, Nourishment, Vitality, Writing, Well-being, Freeing Mental Blocks, and Logic.

Yellow Correspondences

Higher Powers: Solar Energies and Solar, Deities, Knowledge Deities and Travel Deities

Element: Fire and Air

Day of the Week: Sunday

Seasons: Spring Summer and Autumn

Time of the Year: Imbolc, Ostara, Beltane, Litha, Lughnasadh and Mabon

Zodiac: Aquarius, Cancer, Gemini, Leo, Virgo, Libra and Sagittarius

Planets: The Sun and Mercury

Chakra: Solar Plexus Chakra

The Body: Digestion, Liver, Lower Back, Stomach Complains, Menstrual Cramps, Mental Healing and the Spleen

Magical Attributes: Clairvoyance, Divination, Mental Clarity and Logic.

Yellow Crystals

Yellow Crystals can Include: Citrine, Yellow Jasper, Honey Calcite, Amblygonite, Anatase, Sunshine Aura Quartz, Astrophyllite, Anxite-Mangano, Heliodor, Brazillianite, Angelwing Calcite, Cancrinite, Chrysoberyl, Datolite, Yellow Diamond, Golden Enstatite, Yellow Fluorite, Grossularite Garnet, Hanksite, Her desire, Yellow Jade, Yellow Flash Opal, Opriment, Petalite, Citrine Spirit Quartz, Yellow Quartz, Golden Healer, Golden Scapolite, Schalenblende, Sectarian, Sphalerite, Stellerite, Sulphur, Titanite, Imperial Topaz, Yellow Topaz, Vesuvianite, Zincite, Zircon.

Yellow Crystals can also be used for;

(LIGHT YELLOW) Increasing Alertness, Becoming More Aware, Better Communication, Better Organisation, Dealing with Thoughtlessness.

(YELLOW) Enlightenment, Optimism, Realism, Warmth, Dealing with Harshness.

(DARK YELLOW) Constructive Thought Decisiveness, Free Expression, Persuasiveness, Precision, Success in Sales/Selling, Verbalising Needs, Overcoming Misconceptions, Revealing Self-Deceit.

About the Colour Yellow

Yellow is the lightest and brightest of the visible spectrum and is the lightest of the warm colours too. Yellow is the colour that is associated with the midday sun. It's a colour that brings hope, happiness and joy while uplifting and illuminating your way.

Yellow is open-minded and inspiring. Yellow is the colour of the mind and intellect. It's the colour of mental creativity, new ideas and thinking outside the box. Yellow is the colour to turn to when you need to find new ways of doing things. Yellow is very much the thinker rather than a dreamer. Yellow loves a challenge especially if it is a brain teaser, or something that will give your mental muscles a workout. Yellow energy frequencies are able to aid with making decisions of all kinds. Yellow is a fantastic communicator who loves to talk, and the talking is rarely frivolous or pointless. Yellow is always taking everything in and when you to make a decision you can use Yellow to filter what information is important and relevant what is not. Yellow can make you over analytical if used too much; it can make you critical of yourself and others. Yellow is the most visible colour of the visual spectrum and as such has been used with warnings signs as yellow is the easiest colour to see. If you are going through a lot of changes you may find that you aren't too fond of yellow, this is because yellow is vibrating a little too high for you to process it properly.

• Yellow is the colour of intellectuals and stimulates the mental faculties

• Yellow is the colour of uplifting spirits and can awaken greater confidence and optimism.

• Yellow is the colour of new ideas and creative thinking.

• Yellow is the colour of the light of the morning and midday sun, stimulating and enlivening

• Yellow enriches, lightens and activates many of the body's functions

• Yellow flowers and lemons are an instant reminder of the sun's life-giving and life-sustaining energies.

Bring Yellow into your life when:

• There is confusion and indecision

• There is fear and anxiety due to the unknown

• If you have a weakened immune system

• You have a poor memory or find you have trouble concentrating

• You suffer with Seasonal Affective Disorder (SAD)

• Use yellow when are working on a computer. You could use a yellow mouse mat to improve your concentration and help you to stay alert.

The Colour Green

Keywords:

The Psychological meanings of the Green are, Balance, Nature, the Environment, Awareness, Growth, Greed, Envy Renewal, Freshness, Restful, Restoration, Luck, Money, Spring and New Beginnings. The Esoteric meanings of the colour Green are, Abundance, Calm, Agriculture, Generosity, Change, Herbs and Herbal Magic, Healing, Health, Good Fortune, Luck, Longevity, Peace, the Fae, Hope, Money, Druid Magic, Nature Magic, Grounding, Emotional Balance, Immortality, Sowing Seeds, Planting, Prosperity, Strength, Success, Harvests Rebirth, Purification and Transformations.

Green Correspondences

Higher Powers: Earth Goddesses, the Fae, the Green Man and Cernunnos, Fertility Deities, the Horned God and Deities associated with Regeneration/Rejuvenation.

Element: Earth

Days of the Week: Wednesday, Thursday and Friday

Time of the Year: Imbolc, Ostara, Beltane, Litha, Lughnasadh, Mabon, Samhain and Yule

Zodiac: Taurus, Gemini, Cancer, Virgo, Leo, Libra, Sagittarius, Aquarius and Pisces

Planets: Mercury, Venus, Earth

Chakra: The Heart Chakra

The Body: The Heart, Chest, Lungs, Physical Healing, Spine, Upper Back and Healing Nervousness.

Magical Attributes: Luck, Money, Abundance and Prosperity Spells. Spells for New Beginnings. Earth related Spells. Planting Seeds and Growth.

Green Crystals

Green Crystals can include: Dyed Green Agate, Agrellite, Green Tourmaline, Ajoite, Watermelon Tourmaline, Alexandrite, Tremolite, Amazonite, Triphylite, Green Amethyst, Green Apatite, Apophylite, Tsavorite, Atacamite, Unakite, Atlantisite, Varisite, Green Serpentine, Apple Aura Quartz, Aventurine, Vesuvianite, Baryte, Vivianite, Bloodstone, Wavelite, Boracite, Zoisite, Brazilianite, Zincite, Brucite, Zircon, Green Calcite, Cerussite, Chrysoprase, Chlorite (in Quartz), Chrysoveryl, Chrysocolla, Chrysotile, Clinoclase, Diopside, Dioptase, Emerald, Epidote, Green Fluorite, Fuschite, Aegirine, Galaxyite, Grossular Garnet, Uvarovite Garnet, Gaspeite, Talc, Gypsum, Smithsonite, Green Goldstone, Heulandite, Richerite, Hiddenite, Sesame Stone, Jade, Serpentine, New Jade, Seaphinite, Ocean Jasper, Kambaba Jasper, Kiwi Jasper, Titanite, Dragonsblood Jasper, Moss Agate, Green Tiger's Eye, Tree Agate, Green Onyx, Tree Jasper, Peridot,

Kammerite, Ovaline, Green Kyanite, Prasiolite, Labradorite, Prehinite, Lakelandite, Presli Blue Stone, Malachite, Rhyolite, Mariposite, Ruby in Fuschite, Ruby in Zoisite, Moldavite.

Green Crystals can also be used for:

(LIGHT GREEN) - Gentle Growth, Idealism, Merit, Spiritual Development, Strength of Character, Overcoming Jealousy.

(GREEN) - Babies, Creation, Fertility, Growth, New Beginnings, Nurturing, Potency, Productivity, Progress, Rehabilitation, Renewal, Youth, Avoiding Sickness.

(DARK GREEN) - Abundance, Carefulness, Good Fortune, Good Financials, Good Health, Justice, Material Comfort, Money, Physical Growth, Profit, Riches, Safety, Shelter, Survival, Wealth, Wildlife, Overcoming fear.

(LIGHT OLIVE GREEN) - Concentration, Determination, Diligence, Discipline, Endurance, Motivation, Perseverance, Resistance, Easing Failure.

(OLIVE GREEN) - Awakening, Change, Enhanced Listening Skills, Independence, Finding Meaning, Receptiveness, Regeneration, and Sense of Worth, Dealing with Despondency.

(DARK OLIVE GREEN) - Capability, Self-Development, Better Grades, Learning, Problem Solving, Success in School, Curing Ignorance.

About the Colour Green

Green is the middle point of the visual spectrum and is closely connected to balance, harmony and nature. In nature green has a dual meaning or purpose, it's the colour of new growth that appears in the Spring, but it's also the colour of mould that appears on rotting vegetation, or food in the process of decay. It's important to remember that death and decay are vital to keeping nature in balance.

Green can restore and renew energy that has been depleted. Green energy can offer a haven away from the stress of modern day living; it helps us to return to a natural state of balance. This soothing and relaxing quality is why for over three hundred years theatres and not film and TV studios provide an area for actors to relax, and this sanctuary is called 'the Green Room'. Green is a colour that has a strong moral compass and always looks at problems and situations from all sides before making a decision. Green is a combination of the mental clarity and optimism with the calm insight of blue, green has a unique blend inspiring hope and generosity of spirit; this isn't found in any other colour in the spectrum. Green relates to prosperity, abundance, success, and finance and material wealth. With this green has a strong relation to stability, safety and security.

• Green has very strong ties to growth and renewal.

• Green inspires hope, the anticipation of what is to come.

• Green is a powerful colour to promote balance and harmony in all areas of your life.

• Green helps to relax emotional and physical tensions, surrounding yourself with natural greenery will help you to 'get away' for a while

• The need to grow, to expand is one of the core qualities of Green energy.

• If you live in a very urban area having a garden or a room in your home where you can grow plants and flowers will help you to stay grounded and connected to nature.

Bring Green into your life when:

• There is a feeling of restriction or of being confined.

• There is a feeling that something has to change.

• There is a lack of new or fresh ideas

• There is a feeling of being surrounded by overly dominating people in your relationships

Use green when you are feeling restricted or feeling trapped by outside forces. Surrounding yourself with green by taking a walk somewhere naturally green to restore your equilibrium.

The Colour Blue

Keywords:

The Psychological meaning of the colour Blue is Electricity, Energy, High Spirits, Water, Calm, Serenity and Relaxation. The Esoteric meaning of the colour Blue are, Ceremonial Magic, Calm, Charity Emotional Control, Clarity, Energy, Fidelity, Inner Light, Forgiveness, Harmony, Grounding, Honour, Depression, Deep Emotions, Higher Education, Power, Politics, Ocean, Water Magic, Philosophy, Law Enforcement, Truth, Understanding, Sincerity, Serenity, Meditation, Philosophy, Relaxation, Loyalty, Luck, Communication, Spiritual Inspiration, Religion, Researching and Study.

Blue Correspondences

Higher Powers: Earth Goddesses, Wisdom Deities and Sky Gods and Goddesses

Elements: Water and Air

Day of the Week: Thursday and Saturday

Time of the Year: Imbolc, Beltane, Litha, Lughnasadh, Samhain and Yule

Zodiac: Aquarius, Capricorn, Gemini and Libra

Planets: Earth and Jupiter

Chakra: The Throat Chakra

The Body: Neck, Throat, Thyroid, Lungs and Ears

Magical Attributes: Astral Projection, Occult and Spiritual Wisdom and Prophetic Dreams

Blue Crystals

Blue Crystals include: Blue Lace Agate, Ajote, Angelina, Aquamarine, Blue Aragonite, Azirote, Blue Barite, Celestite, Blue Chalcenony, Chrysocolla, Dumortierite, Blue Fluorite, Hemimorphite, Kyanite, Lapis Lazuli, Karimor, Pietersite, Smithsonite, Sodalite, Blue Topaz, Blue Tourmaline, Blue Obsidian, Apatite, Blue Calcite, Tanzanite, Blue Opal, Blue Siderite, Aqua Aura Quartz, Blue Tiger's Eye, Presli Blue stone, Iolite, Papagoite, Sapphire, Chalcanthite and Cavansite.

Blue Crystals can be used for:

(BLUE) Trust, Spiritual Cleaning, Maintaining Belief, Being Conservative, Being Faithful, Obedience, Establishing Order, Loving Pets Better, Being Sincere and Overcoming Insecurity.

(LIGHT BLUE) Absolution, Acceptance, Facing Reality, Immorality, Mellowness, Mildness, Patience, Reconciliation, Dealing with Guilt and Recovery.

(DARK BLUE) Charity, Compassion, Consideration, Discretion, Gentleness, Honour, Humanity, Respect, Sensitivity, Service, Tenderness, Thoughtfulness and a Cure for Disrespect.

About the Colour Blue

Blue is the start of the cooler of the spectrum, and in nature blue surrounds us in the form of the vast expanse of the sky. Blue is the colour which relates to trust, honesty, responsibility and loyalty. Blue is a reliable and dependable colour that also displays confidence and conviction.

Blue is a colour that seeks peace and tranquillity to promote physical and mental relaxation; blue will strive for this above all else. Blue is a bit of a stress reliever, creating a sense of calm and order. Blue is the ultimate communicator, whether it is on a one-to-one basis or as a public speaker. It's the colour of truth and honesty, blue helps you to express yourself with your own truth. The wisdom of the Blue energy comes from higher states of consciousness, allowing different spiritual perspectives. Blue is the colour of spiritual and religious study, it helps contemplation and prayer. Blue is the selfless helper, the rescuer, it's always the giver. Blue energies like to build quality relationships.

• Blue is a safe and non-threatening colour which could be why it's one of the most universally liked colours

• Blue is a colour is orderly and predictable; it prefers to analyse situations before taking action

• Blue is a colour that enhances both wisdom and intellect.

• Blue is peaceful and restful, allowing a sense of calm to wash over you

• Blues that are found in nature help to free the mind from hectic day-to-day life.

• When creating space for peace and relaxation Blue will help you find the goal of quiet contemplation

• Blue is a colour that is related to many compassionate religious figures – The Virgin Mary is predominately depicted wearing darker blue robes. This signifies her authority and importance, but also the ability to hear and respond to the prayers of believers.

Bring Blue into your life when:

• There is a lack of peace and calm

• There is a need to communicate clearly and honestly

• There is a need to assimilate information and see with wise eyes

• There is a need for detachment and solitude

• There is a need for help relating to spiritual or religious studies.

The Colour Indigo

Keywords:

The Psychological meanings of the colour Indigo are; Concentration, Authority, Clarification, Strength, Introspection, Confidence, Clarification, Loyalty, Service and Professionalism. The Esoteric meanings of the colour Indigo are; Balancing Karma, Ambition, Healing, Ceremonial Magic, Meditation, Deep Secrets, Tranquillity, Truth, Spirituality, Defence, Passion, Night, Peace, Religion, Wisdom, Understanding, Justice, Intuition, Dignity, Devotion, Spiritual Inspiration and Idealism.

Indigo Correspondences

Higher Powers: Angels and Angelic Energies

Day of the Week: Wednesday and Saturday

Time of the Year, Mabon, Samhain and Yule

Zodiac: Virgo and Capricorn

Planets: Venus and Saturn

Chakra: Third Eye/Brow Chakra

The Body: The Pineal Gland, Deafness, Dementia, Depression, Vertigo and Phobias

Indigo Crystals

Indigo Crystals can include; Blue Tiger's Eye, Blue Fluorite, Blue John Fluorite (pictured), Kyanite, Pariba Tourmaline, Star Sapphire, London Blue Topaz, Blue Aventurine, Euclase, Indicolite, Darker Hues of Chalcedony, Cavansite, Dumortierite, Venus Fluorite, Andean Opal, Plancheite, Indigo Gabbro, Tanzanite, Sodalite, Lapis Lazuli, Azurite, Apatite, Blue Goldstone, Dark Blue Agate, Iolite, Shattuckite, Labradorite, Sapphire, Blue Spinel, Blue Tourmaline, Blue Aragonite, Benitoite, Hauyne, Lazulite, Chrysocolla, Boulder Opal, Lazulite Quartz.

Indigo Crystals can also be used for:

(LIGHT INDIGO) - Appreciation, Dignity, Fastidiousness, Goodness, Humility, Modesty, Thankfulness, Virtue.

(INDIGO) - Experience, Judgement, Long Life, Maturity, Prestige, Avoiding Foolishness.

(DARK INDIGO) - Morality, Protection from Harm, Religious Mastery, Spiritual Guidance, Spiritual Wealth, Truth, Revealing Lies, Avoiding Tricks, Avoiding Misrepresentation.

About the Colour Indigo

Indigo is a deep and rich colour that is a combination of blue and violet; it is a great colour for working on enhancing your intuition or working on seeing perceptions for what they are. Indigo is closely associated with the Brow Chakra, helping to activate and open your third eye, allowing you to see what is beyond when you are shown, or told.

Indigo is a dignified colour with high aspirations. Indigo is a colour that exudes a sense of deep contemplation and introspection; it's a fantastic colour during meditation as it will help you to achieve higher levels of consciousness. It is very 'new age colour' as it allows you to connect to the higher realms letting you use intuition that is beyond that of the gut feeling intuition. Indigo reflects a state of fairness and impartiality but also has a great devotion to causes. It is the defender of people's rights, and always fights for the underdog, until the end. Indigo is a very structured colour, going to pieces if this isn't structure in place; with this Indigo is strongly connected to ritual, tradition, religion and spiritual practices. Indigo helps spatial awareness, activating the right side of the brain the home of the creative centre of the brain.

• Indigo is the colour related to deep sincerity, and this is one of the greatest qualities.

• When you are looking to add some order in your life, Indigo's love of structure is fantastic.

• Indigo is associated with spiritual wisdom rather than intellectual wisdom.

• Indigo is a conformist colour, it loves ritualised behaviour that have worked in the past.

• Indigo can help people with addictions or addictive personalities.

• Indigo is reminiscent of the midnight sky on a moonless night.

• In the Ancient world Indigo was made from powered Azurite or Lapis Lazuli

• Indigo foods include Blueberries and Sloes.

• When using Indigo to raise your state of awareness, the mind becomes unperturbed by thoughts that come and go.

Bring Indigo into your life when:

• There is a need to focus on personal growth

• There is a need to develop sensitivity skills

• There is a need to quieten mental processes or an overly-chatty mind.

• There is a need to relieve pain, especially mental and emotional.

• There is a lack of understanding of new concepts or ideas.

• There is a need for solitude to deal with personal situations

Use Indigo when you feel a need to find peace so you can reflect. Go outside and take a look up at the night sky. The sky at night allows meditation and deep contemplation to come; it's also a great time where many draw inspiration from.

The Colour Purple/Violet

Keywords:

The Psychological meanings of Purple are Contemplation, Meditation, Imagination, Spirituality, Mystery, Introspection, Richness, Royalty and Vision. The Esoteric meanings of Purple are, Ancient Wisdom, Compassion, Breaking Bad Luck, Confidence, Education, Protection, Spirituality, Meditation, Higher Consciousness, Hidden Knowledge or Messages, Friendship, Progress, Inner Peace, Purification, Protection, Intuition, Intelligence, Religion, Devotion, Leadership, Strength, Study, Learning Secrets, the Occult, Wisdom, Writing, Peace, Passion, Humility, Humble, Justice, Mysteries, Night Magic and Emotional Healing.

Purple Correspondences

Higher Power: Angels, Calling on Ancient Deities, Contact with the Spirit World

Element: Spirit, Aether, Akasha, Ether

Days of the Week: Wednesday, Thursday and Saturday

Time of the Year: Beltane, Samhain and Yule

Chakra: The Crown Chakra

The Body: The Head, Ears, Eyes, Mental Health, the Nervous System, Insomnia and other Sleep Disorders.

Magical Attributes: Clairvoyance, Divination, Spiritual Healing, Astral Projection and Using the Third Eye

Purple & Violet Crystals

Violet Crystals include; Prairie Tanzanite, Grape Chalcenony, Rhodolite Garnets, Violet Hued Rubellite, Cacoxenite, Dyed Violet/Purple Agate,

Alexandrite, Amethyst, Chevron Amethyst, Vera Cruz Amethyst, Violet Spirit Quartz, Ametrine, Violet Apatite, Purple Stichtite (Atlantisite) Lavender Aura Quartz, Charoite, Diopside, Dumortierite, Erythrite, Purple Fluorite, Hackmanite, Iolite, Dyed Purple/Lilac/Lavender Jade, Kammererite, Kunzite, Lepidolite, Violet/Purple/Lilac Opal, Purpurite, Brandberg Amethyst, Purple/Violet Sapphire, Smithsonite, Lavender Spinel, Super Six, Super Seven, Tanzanite, Violet Flame Opal, Vesuvianite, Purple Variscite, Purple Zoisite.

Violet and Purple coloured Crystals can also be used for:

(LIGHT VIOLET) Imagination, Elegance, Ingeniousness, and Luxury

(VIOLET) Following Your Heart, Inspiration, Intuition and Music.

(DARK VIOLET) Answers to the Mysterious, Destiny, Vivid Dreams, Enchantment, Good Luck, Magic, Mystical Beings, Soothing Nightmares.

About the Colour Purple

Purple is a mixture of Red and Blue and share the qualities of the Violet Ray

Violet is the colour with the shortest wavelength but also has the highest energy frequency; it appears in a small band before the frequencies go beyond what we are capable of seeing. Violet and purple are colours of spirituality and imagination. It stimulates our ability to connect to higher realms and higher levels of consciousness.

Violet and purple are a combination of the fluid feminine energies of blue with the raw masculine energies of red, making Violet a balance of the two opposing types of energy. There is a slight difference between Violet and Purple, with Violet appearing in this visual spectrum while Purple is a mixture of blue and red making it slightly darker than violet. Though different in shade both Violet and Purple both contain both types of energies making them a balance of body and spirit. Violet is related to spiritual pursuits and the fulfilment they will eventually bring. Violet expands your awareness, connecting you to higher realms and consciousness's, this has given Violet associations with the transformation of the soul. Violet is a colour that inspires love that is utterly devoid of ego; it encourages sensitivity and compassion. Violet encourages creativity in all its forms. It likes to be original and unique; many creative people are inspired by Violet and they often stand out, proud of their uniqueness.

• Violet is associated with kindness, compassion and love, all are key traits of an Empath.

• Violet is a deeply passionate colour, but unlike the Red energy it prefers to show this more in private rather than public displays

• Violet is a very dignified colour, but is also modest, making Violet a very appealing colour.

• Violet is an acutely spiritual colour that can assist you during meditation, prayer or contemplation

• Meditation spaces will benefit from Violet energy

• Violet and purple are connected to luxury, wealth, royalty and was one of the most expensive colours to make in the past.

Bring Violet into your life when:

• There is a need for balance in your life

• There is a need for the healing process to be sped up

• There is a need to tailor your creativity to apply it for practical purposes

• There is an obstacle that needs removing from your life.

• There is a need to calm over-excited energies

• There is a need to energise lethargy or depression

• There is a need for healing energies

• There is a lack of control over the Crown Chakra

**Use Violet by combining Amethyst and Lavender if you have restless nights or suffer with bouts of Insomnia.

Other Colours, Hues and Shades

In the previous pages I looked at each of the colours of the visible spectrum but there are more colours that are created from differing amounts of pigmented colour or frequency. In this section I will look at colours such as Turquoise, Magenta, Pink, Gold, Silver and Brown, and shades and hues of the varying colours such as Black, White, Lime Green, Terracotta, Sage Green, Ivory, Topaz and Lavender. Each variation of the visible spectrum has its own meaning along with the properties of the core colour that is present. When you look at the different shades of a colour – Purple for example – you can look at in two ways. The first is as an artist would look at the combination of pigments that are mixed together. Second is to look at from a scientist where the varying is a combination of energies frequencies reacting with the eye.

The Colour Turquoise

Keywords:

The Psychological meanings of Turquoise are; Compassion, Confidence, Cool, Calm, Collected, Faithful, Eternity and Infinity, the Seas and Oceans, Serenity, Protection, Water, the Sky Sophistication and Class. The Esoteric meanings of the colour Turquoise are; Attraction, Alteration, Love, Awareness, Change, Clear Thinking, Luck, Logic, Meditation, Calm, Healing, Fertility, Original, Intellectual, Intuitive, Renewal, Rebirth and Social Delight.

Turquoise Correspondences

Higher Power: Water Deities and Energies

Element: Water

Day of the Week: Thursday

Time of the Year: Ostara, Litha - the Spring and Summer

Zodiac - Cancer, Virgo, Scorpio, Aquarius and Pisces

Heavenly Bodies: The Moon and Venus

Chakra: The Controversial Thymus Chakra - between the Heart and Throat Chakras

The Body: The Eyes.

Magical Attributes: Astral Travel, Meditation, Water Magic.

Turquoise Crystals

Turquoise crystals can include; Aqua Aura Quartz, Chrysocolla, Amazonite, Ajote, Deeper Shades of Aquamarine, Deeper Shades of Blue Baryte, Boracite, Bauxite, Clinoclase, Footage, Venus Fluorite, Hemimorphite, Larimar, Blue Andean Opal, Shattuckite, Turquoise, Blue Topaz, Blue Obsidian.

Turquoise Crystals can also be used for;

(LIGHT TURQUOISE) Brotherhood, Harmony, Inner Peace of Mind, Solitude, Tranquillity, Understanding, Dealing with Aggression, Neutralizing Anger, Overcoming Conflict, Fighting Cruelty, Dealing with Rage

(TURQUOISE) Balance, Calmness, Discovery, Emotional Control, Equilibrium, Recovery of Memories, Relaxation, Rest, Self-Awareness, Serenity, Stability, Temperance, Tolerance, Overcoming Anxiety, Dealing with Stress, Losing Undesired Weight.

(DARK TURQUOISE) Adaption, Empathy, Flexibility, Greater Openness, Gaining Perspective, Growing Inner Strength, Practicality, Reducing Irritability.

About the Colour Turquoise

Turquoise is a mixture of blue and green, it bridges the gap between the warm and cool colours of the visible spectrum. Turquoise is the heart communication, clarity and like it bridges the gap between warm and cool it bridges the gap between the heart and the mind.

Turquoise is a happy and friendly colour that always loves life, and even though the energy of Turquoise can lead you on a bit of a roller coaster it always regains its own balance. There is a touch of yellow in Turquoise which lifts up the colour while retaining the tranquillity of blue as well as the growth of green. Turquoise embodies them all recharging your spirits when you are going through stressful times. If there is an emergency, Turquoise is a go-to colour as it allows cooler heads to prevail. It's also a colour that increases sensitivity; it's an influencer rather than a preacher. Turquoise is a very creative colour but it can easily become bored if it's forced to focus on one thing for too long – however it is a fantastic multi-tasking colour. Turquoise is an observer, taking everything in, allowing a way forward to ne found by weighing up all of the pros and cons before a decision is made. It is a wonderful colour to utilise of you is stuck in a rut or feels lost, unsure of which way to go.

• Turquoise helps to facilitate clear and open communication between the head and the heart, allowing thoughts and feelings being shared openly and easily.

• Turquoise is roughly the mid-point between Red – the body – and Violet – the spirit – for this reason Turquoise is a great balancing force.

• Turquoise is an invigorating colour while still being a cool customer

• Turquoise is a self-sufficient colour; it can tap in to itself to discover what it needs, find its own way to success.

• Turquoise enhances your ability to concentrate and focus, its love of order and structure helps with this.

The Colour Pink

Keywords:

The Psychological meanings of the colour Pink are Affection, Compassion, Delicacy Gentleness, Fragile, Romance, Softness, Memory, Nostalgia Youth and Tenderness. The Esoteric meanings of the colour Pink are, Affection, Action, Forgiveness, Healing, Femininity, Feminine Energies, Joy, Harmony, Friendship, Pure Love, Compassion, Innocence, Nurturing, Open Heart, Emotionally Mature, Honour, New Beginnings, Gentle Aspects of Love and Passion, Gentle Strength, Universal Love, Luck, Morals, Spiritual Awakening, Spiritual Healings and Spiritual Love.

Pink Correspondences

Higher Powers: Gods and Goddesses associated with Love and Spiritual Healing

Days of the Week: Tuesday and Friday

Time of the Year: Imbolc, Ostara and Beltane - the Spring

Zodiac: Taurus, Venus and Libra

Planets: Venus and Mars Influences

Chakra: Pink is associated with the Heart Chakra

The Body: Helps with Depression and Anxiety, Breast Cancer, the Heart, Energy and Surgeries

Magical Attributes: Higher Self, Mystic and Mystical Gifts and Achieving Goals and Purposes of Spells.

About the Colour Pink

The colour Pink is a combination of Red and White in varying degrees. The kind of energy you have will depend on how much red energy is present compared to the amount of white energy. White is a representation of completion and fullness. Red is a powerful motivator and will strive to reach its goal. The deeper the pink the more passionate and energetic it is.

Pink is the colour of unconditional love in all its forms and a very nurturing energy. Pink is a compassionate and understanding colour, but it is far more too – it's a romantic and affectionate, thoughtful and caring. White tones down the raw primal physicality, replacing it with a gentle, sensitive and loving energy. Pink is a fantastically intuitive colour using it's empathy to guide it to its desired goal. Pink is a positive colour inspiring warmth and a feeling that everything will be okay, not matter how hard things may get. The colour Pink represents the innocence of children, but also the innocence that we all have inside. It's the colour is simple and uncomplicated emotions. It is a colour that is sometimes associated with naiveté and inexperience. Pink is a non-threatening colour seeking respect, and it's a colour that likes to feel appreciated.

• Pink is the epitome of unconditional of love, romance and devotion.

• Pink is a very compassionate, it's driven by its empathy and to nurture others.

• Pink is often associated with hope and the possible positive outcomes.

• Pink can help can emotional energies that are out of control.

• Pink is the most sensitive of all the colours, it is the epitome of TLC – Tender Loving Care

• Pink is associated with young girls and childhood. A time before the trials and tribulations of life begins to take its toll.

The Colour Magenta

Keywords:

The Psychological meanings of Magenta are; Attention-Getting, Excitement, Festivity, Flirtation, Heat, Playfulness, Sensuality, Stimulating, Theatrical, Wildness. The Esoteric meanings of Magenta are; Attracting or Speeding up Results, Exorcism, Extra Power, Life Path, Life Purpose, Magnetism, Quick Changes, and Spiritual Healing.

Magenta Correspondences

Days of the Week: Wednesday

Zodiac: Scorpio, Capricorn, Pisces

Chakra: Soul Star

Magical Attributes: High Vibrational Frequency, Power, Connecting the Upper and Lower Chakras.

** Magenta has a high vibration and can help to ward off energy vampires. Magenta work quickly and will expedite spells or ritual work.

Magenta Crystals

Fluorite, Ruby, Zircon, Pink Tourmaline, Rhodonite, Spinel, Pink Topaz, Rhodolite Garnet, Colbatic Calcite, Roselite, Magenta Lepidolite, Erythrite.

Magenta Crystals can also be used for;

(LIGHT MAGENTA) Vision, Akashic Inspiration, Creativity, Hidden Knowledge, Inventive, Originality, Poetry, Imagination, Stimulation, Subtlety, Visualisation, Dispelling Illusions.

(DARK MAGENTA) Clear Sight, Discernment, Making Good Decisions, Insight, Perception, Seeing the Future.

About the Colour Magenta

Magenta is created by mixing Red and Violet; even though these colours sit at either end of the visible spectrum but together they combine the passion and energy of red with the quiet introspection of Violet. This means that Magenta has the influence over physical and spiritual development.

Magenta is an instrument of change and is a herald of transformation. It will help to release old fears, behaviours and emotions. It'll help you to release things that are hindering your personal advancement and spiritual development. Magenta helps to create harmony and balance in almost every area of your life and during difficult times Magenta helps to lift our spirits above happiness, anger, hate and frustration. Malachite is a colour many associate with happiness, appreciation, cheerfulness. It promotes compassion and kindness while encouraging self-respect. It's a strong and inspiring colour. At times it can be a colour that is related to the outrageous, the creative and the inventive. It's impulsive, spontaneous while still remaining organised. Magenta is resourceful often turning to innovation and creative ways with problem solving.

- Magenta generates universal love, kindness and caring energy.
- Magenta encourages harmony and balance
- Magenta is the colour of the free spirit
- Magenta is a powerful force for change and transformation.
- Magenta is practical and spiritual at the same time
- Magenta is caring, compassionate and gentle when approaching situations.
- Magenta inspires optimism and cheerful energies as well as creativity and innovation.

The Colour Brown

Keywords:

The Psychological meanings of the colour Brown are Durable, Grounded, Natural, Nature, Outdoors, Richness, Robustness, Deep Rooted, Security, Shelter, Solidarity, Steady, Warm, Wholesome and Wood. The Esoteric meanings of the colour Brown are Animal Healing, Animal Magic, Financial Success, Balanced, Family, Grounding, Hard Work, Learning, Health, Intuition Conservation, Craftsmanship, Protection, Strength, Study, Strength, Wealth, Effort, Concentration, Livestock, Empathy and Druidry.

Brown Correspondences

Higher Powers: Mother Nature, Gaia, Nature deities such as Cernunnos.

Element: Earth

Days of the Week: Monday and Friday

Time of the Year: Imbolc, Lughnasadh, Mabon and Samhain.

Zodiac: Taurus, Virgo, Scorpio, Sagittarius and Capricorn

Planets: Venus, Earth and the Moon

Magical Attributes: Extra Sensory Perception, Intuition Enhancement and Psychic Abilities.

Brown Crystals

Brown Crystals can include: Smoky Quartz, Petrified Wood, Picture Jasper, Turritella Agate, Spessartine Garnet, Leopardskin Jasper, Bruno Jasper, Stromatolite, Botswana Agate, Natural

Agate, Amber, Anatase, Andalusite, Asteophyllite,
Axinite - Farro, Axinite - Mangano, Bornite,
Bronzite, Bytownite, Dragons Blood Calcite, Dark
shades of Carnelian, Cassitetite, Modular
Chalcedony, Chiatlstolite, Desert Rose,
Chrysoberyl, Diopside, Dravite, Enstatite,
Franklinite, Fulgurite, Hessonite Garnet,
Herderite, Hureaulite, Tiger Jasper, Ocean Jasper,
Labradorite, Marston Marble, Merlinite, Mica,
Mookaite, Moqui Marbles, Muscovite, Banded
Onyx, Elestial Smoky Quartz, Rhyolite, Richerite,
Sardonyx, Septarian, Smithsonite, Sunstone,
Super Six, Tiger's Eye, Tiger Iron, Vanandanite,
Vesuvianite, Zircon, Shiva Lingam.

Brown Crystals can also be used for:

Centering, Comfort, Integration, Organisation,
Earth Energies, Soul, Combating Chaos,
Grounding.

About the Colour Brown

Brown is another very nature orientated colour
and is the result of mixing all of the primary
colours together, which gives it the power to blend
in with its surroundings. Brown is a base colour
on which other colour can show off. Brown is a
neutral colour which has no pretence, it is what it
is.

Brown is a very non-threatening colour and
carries a very comfortable and familiar energy,
Brown is a practical colour which it gets from the
red energy, and it's also nimble-minded and has
the mental acuity from the yellow energy with the
addition the soothing and studious blue energy.
Brown is a very structured and stable colour
offering supportive energies. Brown is often
associated with material possessions and material
wealth. Brown is probably one of the most

approachable colours because it has no threatening energies. It's an upfront and honest colour; it doesn't pretend to be anything it isn't. Brown is trustworthy, loyal and dependable; it's a very sensible colour with an acute level of common sense. Brown is a frugal colour; it isn't about excess or extravagance, rather everything in moderation. Brown is a very down to earth colour; it is literally the colour of the Earth – the dirt beneath our feet. It can help to keep you grounded when you are feeling lost or spiralling out of control. Brown has a unique ability to suppress emotions, which allows a calm energy embrace you creating a safe haven.

• Brown is a very stable colour. It's reassuring and comforting.

• Brown is a structured colour, it loves organisation.

• Brown is the most predominant colour on the planet along with green.

• Brown is associated to wholesome, health and nutrition.

• Brown is a very protective colour helping you to feel safe and secure.

• Brown is a comforting colour; it is friendly and approachable for everyone.

The Colour Grey

Keywords:

The psychological meanings of the colour Grey are; Maturity, Detachment, Professionalism, Steadfast, and Enduring. In Esoteric meanings of the colour Grey are; Balance, Banishment, Breaking of Old Habits, Doubt, Negates Negativity, Neutral, Releases Negative Thoughts and Feelings, Stability and Confusion Leading to 'sitting on the fence'.

Grey Correspondences

Element: Fire

Days of the Week: Monday and Saturday

Time of the Year: Imbolc and Yule

Zodiac: Capricorn and Virgo

Planetary Influence: The Moon and Saturn

Magical Attributes: Astral travel, Clairvoyance, and Good for contemplating and complex personal issues through meditation.

Grey Crystals

Botswana Agate, Grey Agate, Satellite, Angelite/Anhydrite, Brucite, Carborundum, Cerussite, Chalcenony, Cuprite, Fulgurite, Galena, Hanksite, Hackmanite, Hypersthene, Iolite, K2 Stone, Labradorite, Larvikite, Lava, Lodestone, Lollingite, Magnetite, Merlinite, Mica, Molybdenite, Muscovite, Presli Bluestone, Sapphirine, Silicon, Stibnite, Tunellite, Ulexite, Zincite, Zircon and Zoisite.

Grey Crystal Can be used for: Feminine Energies, Lunar Energies, Introspection, Coolness, Night Magic, Understanding the Future, Reflection, Quiet, Inner Truth, and Purpose.

About the Colour Grey.

Grey is the true meaning of neutral. Grey is considered to be the mid-point between White and Black. It is the colour of the void, of emptiness. It's the colour that relates to a lack of movement, a lack of emotions. This is what makes Grey such a restful and relaxing colour, because it doesn't have any identifying or unique characteristics.

Grey allows you to take a real break from what is adding pressure in your life. Grey has a cool, calm and collected with a calculating mind. Grey is a calming colour to the point it can be considered to be detached, distant and filled with indecision. Grey is often as an "on the fence" colour because of its strong neutral energy. Grey is the colour of compromise – Grey is the combination of White and Black, which means it has the pure and tranquil energy of the White with the protective absorbing energy of the Black energy. Grey is a conservative colour and often seen as drab, boring and will go as far as saying Grey is a depressing colour. It is a conventional colour which is always dependable and practical. Grey is a colour that is associated with the elder years of life – the years of the Crone and the Sage. It's not a colour that will take centre stage but it will stand on the outside creating a solid base without being extroverted.

• Grey is a neutral colour it is always impartial, never taking sides.

• Grey is the colour that is closely associated to making compromises.

• It is the colour that lives between White and Black.

• Grey is very indecisive, it prefers to sit on the fence not making decisions.

• Grey is an emotionless or disinterested.

• Grey is a very reserved colour and will steady other colour it is paired with.

The Colour Black

Keywords:

The Psychological Meaning of Black is Bold, Empowerment, Evil, Invulnerable, Magic, Mourning, Strong, Mysterious, Rebellious, and Sobering. The Esoteric Meanings of Black are Absorber of Energy and Negativity, Banishing, Binding, Death, Creation, Confusion, Night Time, Truth, Understanding, Loss, Deeper Consciousness, Totality, Repelling.

Black Correspondences

Higher Powers - The Crone from the Triple Goddess, Underworld Relating Deities such as Hades, Anubis, Osiris and Hella.

Element - Earth

Day of the Week - Saturday

Time of the Year - Imbolc, Samhain and Lughnasadh

Zodiac - Capricorn, Libra and Scorpio

Planet - Saturn

Magical Abilities - Astral Projection and Divination

Black Crystals

Black Crystals can Include: Aegirine, Black Agate, Alabaridite, Black Amethyst, Apache Tear, Anthracite, Brookite, Carborundum, Cassitetite, Chiastolite, Cuprite, Black Diamond, Flowerstone, Franklinite, Melanite Garnet, Hematite, Hypersthene, Irghizite, Jet, Zebra Jasper, Kimberlite, Black Kyanite, Lakelandite, Lava, Magnetite, Marston Marble, Nebula, Nuumite, Obsidian, Onyx, Smoky Quartz, Tibetan Quartz, Tourmlinated Quartz, Sardonyx, Schalenblende, Shungite, Stromatolite, Black Tourmaline, Zircon.

Black Crystals can also be used for:

Mystery, Security Transformation, Grounding, Protection, Cure for Self-Doubt, Mental Fortitude, Focus, Amplify Efforts, Energy Barriers, Relieving Fears, Transmutation

About the Colour Black

The colour Black technically isn't a colour it is an absence of light. It is also the most misunderstood colour having the most misconceptions about it, probably more than all the others colours combined. Black has the same level of positive attributes as it has negative attributes. Black is mysterious, protective, control, discipline and independence.

Black is the opposing force to white, so what White brings to light Black will hide. Black is the absorption of all colours and the absence of light. With this Black is related to the mysterious, all that is hidden, secretive and the unknown. Black has the ability to between us and the outside world, which allows us to feel safe in its embrace, providing protection, Black can hide such things as vulnerability, insecurity and a lack of self-confidence, self-love and self-worth. At some point in our lives we will have instinctively worn or chosen black as a way to blend in, and hide us from the eyes of the world, allowing us to hide things like fears, true feelings and insecurities we feel are paralysing. Black is associated power and control, control over the surroundings or information; refusing to share the information it may have learned. Black can be very unfriendly and intimidating due in part to the power and control aspects. Black absorbs negative energy as easily as it absorbs light; by taking something black with you on your day today travels you can protect yourself from negative energy because the black will absorb the negativity. Black is also associated to seduction and sexiness because it creates an air of mystery making women into temptress. Black is also a colour that implies submission to something or someone. Black is often associated with the end of things. Black is a colour that is linked to sophisticated and successful people. A black tie or little black dress implies affluence, success and influence.

• Black is the colour of mystery, it loves keeping secrets.

• Black hides its true feelings unwilling to share them with others.

• Black is all about power and control whether it be over the self or over others.

• Black can create and air of fear, anxiety and intimidation.

• Black is associated to formality and sophistication which can be embodied by the Black Tie or the Little Black Dress.

• Black is can be very distant, setting itself aside.

• Black can stop us from looking on the positive aspects of life while only focusing on the negative.

The Colour White

Keywords:

The Psychological meanings of White are, Clear, Clean, Airy, Ethereal, Bridal, Shyness, Silent and Sterile. The Esoteric meanings of the colour White are, Purity, Wholeness, Innocence, Virginal, Air Element, Healing, Freedom, Forgiving, Simplicity, Sincerity, Serenity, Wholeness, Truth, Protection, and Perfection.

White Correspondences

Higher Power: Angels, Higher Realms, Spirit Guides, the Gods or Goddesses and the Moon.

Element: Spirit/Ether/Aether/Akasha

Day of the Week: Monday, Tuesday, Thursday, Friday and Saturday

Times of the Year: Imbolc and Yule

Chakra: The Crown Chakra

The Body: Mending of Broken Bones, Dental Pain Aid, and Nursing Mothers.

Magical Attributes: Clairvoyance, Divination, Contacting Higher Realms, Angelic Work, Astral Travel and Shamanic Journeying.

White Crystals

▫ White crystals include both clear and white toned crystals: White/Clear Calcite, Optical Calcite, Angel Aura, Scolecite, White Agate, Howlite, Snow Quartz, Girasol Quartz, Moonstone, White Petalite, White Aragonite, White Coral, Rock Salt, Clear Topaz, Selenite, Clear Quartz, Opalite, Opal, Solar Quartz, Diamond, Achroite Tourmaline, Albite, Beryllonite, Baryte, Dolomite, Pearl, White Jade, Zircon and Danburite.

White Crystals can also be used for:

Cohesiveness, Freedom, Hope, Illumination, Purity, Unity, Remove Inhibitions, Moon Energy, the Spiritual World, and a Guide to Knowledge, Wisdom and Understanding

About the Colour White

White contains equal amounts of each colour in the visible spectrum which creates a sense of completion. This means that white represents

wholeness, completion and perfection. White is
associated with purity, wholeness and innocence.
When we think about White it is the proverbial
clean slate and the blank canvas.

White is the colour of new beginnings and starting
something new allowing us to write our own story,
to express yourself however you wish to. White
isn't really isn't a stimulating colour, but it have to
be; however it opens up the mind and heart to
anything. White represents the dual aspects of
every colour, having both the positive and the
negative there. White is a colour that embodies
characteristics such as fairness, impartiality
independence and balance. White is reflective so
it's a colour you can't hide behind. It will force you
into the light and make you face what you are
trying to hide. White will help to open you up to
creative forces and will amplify energy that it is
exposed to. White is seen world wide as a symbol
of purity and cleanliness. Brides where white as a
symbol of their purity, and doctors will wear white
coats for much the same reasons. Which is also a
protective colour which helps to encourage a sense
of peace and calm? White is a comforting colour
which can help if you are experiencing emotional
difficulties or emotional stress. White is a
cleansing colour, purifying you of negative
thoughts and feelings. Many Spiritual
practitioners will use a visualisation of a White
light as a cleansing force or a protective one in the
form of a bubble of white light. Some cultures see
white as a negative, unemotional and isolated,
while it other cultures see white as a colour of
mourning in the sense that death is the end of one
cycle but also the beginning of a new one. It can
also be used if you feel you are coming to the end
of a phase in your life leading you to wear white.

• White is a symbol of purity and innocence.

• White can represent the beginning of a new
phase in life, indicating a clean slate.

• White can help you put the past behind you by focusing on the here and now

• White is a colour closely associated with unity because White is a combination of all other colours.

• White also represents equality because it contains equal amounts of each colour.

• White doesn't take sides even though it is one side of the polarity scales.

• White is often associated with the fictional rescuer, the White Knight who will battle the forces of darkness and evil.

• When White represents the clean slate it can also mean that it is organised.

The Colour Silver

Keywords:

The Psychological meanings of the colour Silver are; Duty, Efficiency, Logical, Methodical, Neutrality, Practicality, Quiet and Sobriety. The Esoteric meanings of the colour Silver are; Balance, Cancellation, Feminine Energy, Femininity, Goddess Energy, the Moon, Intuition, Meditation, Confidence, Dreams, Harmony, Introspection, Logic, Priestess, Passion, Protection, Rebirth and Reincarnation, Stability, Secrets, Repelling or Removing Negative Energies.

Silver Correspondences

Higher Power: Feminine Energies and Deities, the Goddess and Lunar Energies and Deities

Element: Air

Day of the Week: Monday, Tuesday and Wednesday

Zodiac: Cancer

Planet: The Moon

The Body: Helps with Hormone Imbalances

Magical Attributes: Astral Energies, Divination, Intuition, Clairvoyance and Clairaudience, Increasing Psychic Abilities and Meditation

Silver Crystals

Galena, Hematite, Silver Pyrite (?), Stibnite, Silver, Silver Topaz, Silver Aura Quartz, Chalcedony, Cuprite, Fulgerite, Hanksite, Lollingite, Molybdenite, Muscovite, Schalenblende, Silicon.

Silver Crystals can also be used for:

Feminine Energy, Lunar Energy, Goddess Energy, Introspection, Intuition, Coolness, Night Magic, Understanding the Future, Reflection, Quiet, Inner Truth, Purpose

About the Colour Silver

The colour Silver has a strong feminine energy. Silver is closely with the Moon, and the Goddess figure in many Pagan traditions. Silver is a very fluid colour and its connection to the Moon means that has a certain mystery about it, something you can't quite put your finger on.

Silver is a colour that is associated with soothing energies and has the ability to calm even the most turbulent of energies. One of Silver's strongest attributes is its ability to reflect at your situation; helping you to change your direction. Silver can help to illuminate

* Silver opens the mind allowing you to move forward on the path it has illuminated.

* Silver is a great colour for repelling or reflecting energies back to the sender, both positive and negative energies.

* Silver has an iconic colour for the Feminine Energies and the Moon, Sensitive, Strong and Fluid.

* Silver is a calming and soothing colour, it's a comforting colour bringing a sense of security.

* Silver is a sophisticated and glamorous, almost ethereal nature.

The Colour Gold

Keywords:

The Psychological meanings of the colour Gold are Divine, Divinity, Winning, Prestige, Honour, Radiance, Power, Rich, Wealth, Luxury and Intuition. The Esoteric meanings of the colour Gold are, Authority, Abundance, Wealth, Charm, Charisma, Confidence, Generosity, Justice, Luck, Luxury, Creativity, Intuition, Playfulness, Money, Power, Motivation, Success, Masculine Energy, the Sun, Victory, Wealth, Power, Prosperity, protection, Perfection, Confidence, Happiness and Health.

Gold Correspondences

Higher Power: Male Deities, Masculine Energies and Aspects of the Divine, Solar Energy and Deities.

Element: Fire

Day of the Week: Thursday and Sunday

Time of the Year: Ostara, Beltane, Litha, Lughnasadh and Yule - associated with the strength of the Sun and the Harvests in Autumn

Zodiac: Leo and Virgo

Planet: The Sun with the Cosmic Influences of the Sun

Chakra: The Gods Head Chakra

Magic Attributes: Authority, Self-Confidence, Creativity, Wealth, Prosperity, Investment, Hope, Power and Solar Energy.

Gold Crystals

Rutilated Quartz, Golden Apatite, Golden Calcite, Golden Selenite, Imperial Topaz, Pyrite, Tiger's Eye, Golden Healer, Amber, Citrine, Golden Labradorite, Heliodor Beryl, Ametrine, Golden Aura Quartz, Mangano Axinite, Bronzite, Bytownite, Chrysoberyl, Enstatite, Grossularite Garnet, Spessartine Garnet, Gold, External Rutile, Goldstone (?), Herderite, Karibibite, Schalenblende, Sectarian, Stellerite, Stromatolite, Zircon and Zincite.

Gold Crystals can also be used for:

(LIGHT GOLD) Better Life, Cheerfulness, Confidence, Ecstasy, Engagement, Happiness, Satisfaction, Overcoming Pessimism, Dealing with Sadness.

(GOLD) Adventure, Ambition, Enthusiasm, Excitement, Excellence, Intuition, Liveliness, Travel, Easing Worries.

(DARK GOLD) Authority, Control, Fame, Influence, Fame, Influence, Material Wealth, Power, Feeling Powerful.

About the Colour Gold

By its very nature Gold is a colour that speaks of wealth, success, prestige, achievement and success, and this is the same around the globe in various areas of life. For sports many men and women it is the reward for long hours of hard work in their career; in many competitions around the world, Gold medals are awarded to those who have outshone all of their competitors and won. In the world of money Gold is probably the most traded commodity, as the value of gold is the same globally. Gold is a colour that is associated with Royalty too and the greatest display of this wealth can be found in Crown Jewels from different countries, Britain being among the most famous.

Gold is a masculine energy colour and represents the power, might and strength of the Sun, gold also represents optimism and positive energy as well as warmth. Wearing gold can help bring an optimistic and positive outlook to situations. Gold also has the ability to illuminate routes and solutions to problems; it shows you ways you may not have considered before. Gold is associated with High Ideals, Knowledge and Wisdom, it is also the colour that is sometimes most associated with enlightenment and spiritual advancement. It inspires you to search for answers to understand the self and the soul. It inspires you to search for the meaning in your spiritual path, and how you can move forward with both knowledge and understanding. Gold is a very generous colour; it has a loving, giving and compassionate nature despite the misconceptions of modern society. It is the colour of benefactors and patrons of charities and charitable organisations, and those who employ gold in this manner are passionate about their work. Gold tends to draw the eye so can be used to illuminate problems, or show what may need a little attention or tender loving care.

Gold is a warm colour that tends to be shiny, glittery or metallic. The bright shiny Gold catches the eye with its striking beauty while the deeper shades of gold are warm, homely and intense. Gold can be egotistical in nature, and be unable to trust. If you are surrounded by too much gold you may find that you are drawn toward its negative associations of Greed, Power Hungry and Selfish.

* Gold is a signature colour for wealth, success and achievement.

* Gold is a very prestigious and luxurious colour; it speaks of sophistication and elegance too.

* At Gold's highest frequency is resonates with knowledge, wisdom and enlightenment.

* Gold is a colour that is always searching for the deeper meaning to life's questions.

Metals Correspondences in Magic

Metals can be extremely useful in Witchcraft as it can be used to make magical amulets. Metals act as an amplifier; they increase the power and potency of items. Metals can also help you to focus your intentions of you rituals and spell work. Metal can be used to create wands, runes jewellery that will combine the energies of the metal and a crystal for example. Below is a quick rundown of their correspondences.

Aluminium = Companionship, Safe Travel, Mercurial Energy

Brass = Open-Mindedness, Healing, Wealth, Prosperity, Solar Energy

Bronze = Fairness, Compromise, Solar Energy

Chromium = Compromise, Adaptation, Protection, Repels Negative Energy

Copper = Love, Sensuality, Friendship, Relationships, Pease, Creativity, Attraction, Pain Reliever

Electrum = Action, Movement, Catalyst [Can be DANGEROUS]

Gold = Authority, Self-Confidence, Creativity, Wealth, Prosperity, Investment, Hope, Power, Solar Energy

Iron = protection, Energy, Strength, Determination, Aggression, Power, Courage, Grounding

Lead = Curses, Defensive and Offensive Magic, Banishing, Breaking Bad Habits, Protection, Stability, Grounding

Mercury = Mental Clarity, Intellect, Duality

Nickel = Energy, Manifestation, Protection, Catalyst

Pewter = Divination, Clairvoyance, Intuition, Protection

Platinum = Balance, Meditation, Insight, Foresight, Self-Sacrifice [DANGEROUS]

Plutonium = Transformation, Change

Silver = Neutralising Negativity, Dreams, Intuition, Psychic Work, Lunar Energy

Steel = Defensive Magic, Warding, Protection, Repels Nightmares,

Tin = Abundance, Prosperity, Growth, Success, Mercy

Titanium = Strength, Protection

Uranium = Intuition, Freedom, Clairvoyance, Discovery [DANGEROUS]

Zinc = Transformation, Revelation, Growth, Protection

Section 8 – References & Suggestions

Through the process of researching this Almanac, and through the articles I write for Ramblings of a Rainbow Witch and Magical Recipes Online. This is a collection of websites, books and Facebook pages that I have either used in this research, or suggest taking a look at.

Websites

- www.lunarium.co.uk
- www.findyourfate.com
- www.goldenchennai.com
- www.moonconnection.com
- http://home.hiwaay.net
- www.groveandgrotto.com
- www.llewellyn.com
- www.suttons.co.uk
- www.witchinghoursociety.com
- www.crystalage.com
- www.crystalvaults.com

- <http://members.tripod.com/kender_witch>
- www.thepaganjourney.weebly.com
- <http://magic-spells-and-potions.com>
- www.shirleytwofeathers.com

Facebook Pages

Ramblings of a Rainbow Witch – Lady Willow's BOS – The Oogie Boogie Witch – By Candle Light – Healing Energy Tools – The Eclectic Witch – The Realm of the Witch – Hoodoo Guru – Hoodoo Delish – Witchy Words – Zodiac Signs – Those Secret Thoughts – Sapphire Moonbeams – Witchy Woman Way – Earthmagick – Witch's Cauldron – Druid's Path – The Nemeton – Spirit de la Lune – To Ride a Broomstick – The Olde Religion – Enchanted Witchery – The Witches Witch – The Pagan Path – Human Odyssey – The Pagan Poppet – Kitchen Witch – Old World Witchcraft – Star Child Glastonbury – The Humorous Witch – La Hermosa Bruja The Beautiful Witch – The Good Witch – Barefoot Kitchen Witch – Wildwoman Sisterhood – Crystal Judy Hall – Eclectic Pagan – Amazing Geologist – The Spellery – The White Witch Parlour – Behind the Purple Door – The Laughing Witch – Witch of Avalon – Black Hat Society – The Domestic Witch – Pagan Lady – The Magical Cottage – The Good Witch's Cottage – The Provocative Witch – If the Broom Fits, Ride it – The Garnet Witch's Grimoire – My Twisted Path – The Discreet Witch – The Wyse Witch – The Deviant Witch – The Mystic Witch- Witchy Witch – The Crazy Witches Journal – The Alder Scrolls – The Goddess Circle – One Million Pagans – The Crystal Witches)O(- Southern Hemisphere Pagan – The Pink Cauldron – Magickbaby's – Magickal Moonie's Sanctuary – Wicca Annie's BOS – The Smart Witch – Confessions of Crafty Witches – Hibiscus Moon – Magical Recipes Online – The Green Witch- Ravensgrove Coven – Raven's Hearth – Pauline

Clynch Clairvoyant – The Oogie Boogie Witch – Daughter of the Goddess – The Frosted Maple Witch – Practical Witch – Red's Safe Haven – Barefoot Five – Chaos Witch and The Crystal Healer.

Books

Ramblings of a Rainbow Witch's 2018 Almanac
The Astrology Bible – Judy Hall
The Wicca Bible – Ann-Marie Gallagher
The crystal Bible 1 & 2 – Judy Hall
The Witch's Companion – Soraya
The Kitchen Witch – Soraya
The Lure of Gems – Steve Bennett
The Witches Datebook – Multiple Authors
The Healing with Colour Manual – Pauline Wills
Healing with Colour – Theo Gimbel
The Beginner's Guide to Colour Psychology – Angela Wright
The Crystal Healer – Phillip Permut
Crystals: Colour and Chakra – Gill Hale
Moon Magic – Lori Reid
Moonology – Yasmin Boland
Colour Therapy Workbook – Theo Gimbel
Egyptian Birthstones – Storm Constantine
Colour Your Life – Howard Sun
Crystal, Gem & Metal Magic – Scott Cunningham
Earth, Air, Fire, Water – Scott Cunningham
Complete Book of Witchcraft – Raymond Buckland
The Goodly Spellbook – High Priestess Lady Passion
The Witches Bible – Janet Farrar
Wiccapedia – Shawn Robbins
The Good Witch's Guide – Shawn Robbins
Wiccapedia Journal – Shawn Robbins
Way of the Goddess – Ann-Marie Gallagher
Way of Shamanism – Leo Rutherford
Way of Natural Magic – Nigel Pennick

Wicca – Scott Cunningham
Living Wicca – Scott Cunningham
The Tarot Bible – Sarah Bartlett
The Mythology Bible – Sarah Bartlett
The Mythological Creatures Bible – Brenda Rosen
Hedgewitch – Rae Beth
Fine your Animal Spirit – David Carson
Spells & Psychic Powers – Soraya
The Book of English Magic – Richard Heygate
The Inner Beauty Bible – Laurey Simmons
Encyclopaedia of Magic & Ancient Wisdom – Cassandra
Easson
Earth Magic – Steven Farmer PhD
Sacred Tree Medicine – Ellen Evert-Hopman
Crystal Healing for Animals – Martin J. Scott
The Green Witch – Arin Murphy-Hiscock
The Art of Mysticism – Gabriyell Sarom
Way of Wicca – Vivianne Crowley
Way of Psychic Protection – Judy Hall
Way of Karma – Judy Hall

Thank you for purchasing this Almanac, your love and
support means the world to me, and I promise to
continue to reach higher, making the Almanac better
and better.